Creative Cookbook Company Presents

D0190673

Compiled by
**Professional Home Economics Teachers
& Family and Consumer Science Teachers
of California, Nevada, Arizona, and Utah**

Editor
Gerry Murry Henderson

Graphic Design, Typography, and Production
Mike Burk Production Services, Long Beach, CA

Library of Congress Catalog
**Card No. 83-072758
ISBN 0-914159-20-8**

2/C3CM0608/MBPS/DPS

Eating BETTER

Thanks to the Home Economics (FACS) Teachers who have compiled their best recipes for Eating Better. Instead of one particular diet, these recipes have lots of variety- low-carb, low-calorie, or simply fresher ingredients. We hope they help you and your family to eat better.

Teacher Advisory Committee

KATHIE BACZYNSKI
Mt. Carmel High School, San Diego, CA

PRISCILLA BURNS
Pleasant Valley High School, Chico, CA

DIANE CASTRO
Temecula Valley High School, Temecula, CA

NEVA CLAUSON
Lebanon High School, Lebanon, OR

DIANE CLUFF
Provo High School, Provo, UT

JAMEY DAVIS
Redwood Int. School, Thousand Oaks, CA

CAROLE DELAP
Golden West High School, Visalia, CA

MARIA FREGULIA
Lassen High School, Susanville, CA

DEBBIE HARVEY
Amador Valley High School, Pleasanton, CA

GERRY HENDERSON
Temple City High School, Temple City, CA

CAMILLE HICKS
Riverton High School, Riverton, UT

KARYN HOBBS
Lemoore High School, Lemoore, CA

REIKO IKKANDA
S. Pasadena Middle School, S. Pasadena, CA

MARY LASH
Paramount High School, Paramount, CA

JAN MARTIN
Reed High School, Sparks, NV

GAIL MCAULEY
Lincoln High School, Stockton, CA

LEILANI NEINER
Mesquite High School, Gilbert, AZ

BETTY RABIN-FUNG
Sierra Vista Jr. High, Canyon Country, CA

APRIL ROSENDAHL
Chino High School, Chino, CA

SONJA SHUMAKER
Ayala High School, Chino Hills, CA

ANNE SILVEIRA
Shasta High School, Redding, CA

KAREN TILSON
Poly High School, Riverside, CA

SUE WATERBURY
San Luis Obispo HS, San Luis Obispo, CA

KATHRYN P. WHITTEN
Home Economics Education, Fresno, CA

Thanks to the following people for working hard to produce a great product:

Gerry Henderson, our editor who carefully checks each recipe to make sure they are perfect. **Betty Rabin-Fung** and **Sue Russell** who spend many hours typing and proofreading the book for accuracy. **Roger Upperman, Ron Rouintree,** and **Jason Medina** who drive long distances to make sure we give the kind of service our customers expect. **Tim Campbell, Marc Trimble,** and **Grady Reed** who help teachers conduct successful sales throughout the Western U.S. **Mike Burk,** our creative designer, who oversees production and layout so our books have such a quality look. **Jerry Bernstein** with **Delta Printing Solutions** who professionally print and bind our books.

A big thanks to the students who sell these books, and finally you the purchaser, for helping provide quality programs in so many schools throughout our communities.

Sincerely,

Doug Herrema and **Doug Pierce,** owners, **Creative Cookbook Company.**

P.S. Please note the re-order form in the back of this book or visit our web site at **www.creativecookbook.com**

Table of CONTENTS

Appetizers & Beverages	5
Breads & Bakery Items	15
Soups, Stews & Chili	26
Salads, Slaws & Dressings	38
Sauces, Salsa & Marinades	56
Vegetables & Side Dishes	59
Main Dish Entreés with...	
Beef	73
Poultry	82
Pork	108
Seafood	111
Meatless	119
Cakes, Cookies & Desserts	126
Index of Contributors	149
Index of Recipes	155
Re-Order Forms	159

Mesquite Chicken Kabobs

Serves: 4

> 1 cup Lawry's Mesquite Marinade with Lime Juice, divided
> 1 pound boneless, skinless chicken breasts, cut into chunks
> 1 (medium) red onion, cut into wedges
> 1 green bell pepper, cored, seeded, cut into 1" chunks
> 12 cherry tomatoes
> 12 mushrooms, cut in half
> 6 (8") skewers

In large resealable plastic bag, combine ³/₄ cup Mesquite Marinade with Lime Juice and remaining ingredients, except skewers. Marinate in refrigerator 1 hour, turning occasionally, discard used marinade. On skewers, thread all ingredients. Grill or broil until chicken is thoroughly cooked, about 15 minutes; brushing often with remaining marinade.

*"Wonderful for picnics and grill parties. For wrap sandwiches,
remove skewers after grilling and serve in flour tortillas."*

Lawry's, Inc.   **Monrovia, CA**

Appetizers & BEVERAGES

Chunky Artichoke Salsa

Makes: 2 cups (2 T each)   *15 Cal; 1g Fat*

1 (6.5 ounce) jar marinated artichoke hearts, drained, chopped
1/4 cup pitted olives, chopped
1 tablespoon red onion, chopped
3 (medium) plum tomatoes, coarsely chopped
1 clove garlic, pressed
2 tablespoons fresh basil, snipped
salt and ground black pepper, to taste

Mix all ingredients in a bowl. Season with salt and pepper. Serve with baked pita chips or crackers.

Pamela Campion   **Dublin High School, Dublin, CA**

Chunky Black Bean Salsa

Makes: 6 cups   *21 Cal. per 1/2 cup*

3 tomatoes, seeded, chopped
1 (15 ounce) can black beans, rinsed, drained
1 jalapeno pepper, seeded, diced
1/2 (small) sweet onion, chopped
1/4 cup fresh cilantro, chopped
1/2 teaspoon lime rind, grated
3 tablespoons fresh lime juice
1/2 teaspoon salt
1/2 teaspoon ground pepper
Baked tortilla chips

Combine first 9 ingredients in bowl; cover and chill until ready to serve. Serve with baked tortilla chips.

"Healthy snacks increase energy levels and boost metabolism. Choose from several different food groups, limiting those high in fat and sugar."

Judy Dobkins   **Redlands High School, Redlands, CA**

Crab Tostadas

Serves: 10 - 15

2 1/2 pounds imitation crab, shredded
1 1/2 to 2 bunches cilantro, chopped
2 bunches green onions, chopped
4 to 6 (large) radishes, diced
1 (large) tomato, seeded, diced
3 fresh green jalapeño peppers, seeded, diced
1 cup fresh lemon juice
crisp tostada shells
Tapatio Mexican hot sauce

Put all ingredients (except tostada shells and hot sauce) in a large bowl and toss lightly. Season with Mexican hot sauce or serve with sauce on the side so everyone can put on their desired amount. Spoon onto tostada shells and serve immediately. Refrigerate leftovers.

"Proportions may be changed according to personal tastes.
We make this is in class every year, and the students love it!"

Sandra Massey   **Mt. View High School, El Monte, CA**

Dill Vegetable Dip

Serves: 6 - 8

1 cup sour cream
1 cup mayonnaise
1 tablespoon parsley
1 tablespoon dried minced onion
1 teaspoon dill weed
1/2 teaspoon Beau Monde seasoning

Mix all ingredients together and chill at least 2 hours (overnight is best). Serve with a variety of fresh vegetables such as asparagus, grape tomatoes, broccoli florets, mushrooms, baby carrots, Chinese pea pods.

Gail McAuley   **Lincoln High School, Stockton, CA**

Fruit Smoothie

Serves: 4

1 cup juice (orange, apple, cranberry)
1 cup nonfat fruit-flavored yogurt
1 cup frozen berries or fresh fruit
   (strawberries, raspberries, banana, oranges, lemons)
1 cup ice
sugar, to taste

Combine all ingredients in blender and blend well.

"Easy! I like to make this with cran-raspberry juice."

Anne Silveira   **Shasta High School, Redding, CA**

Fruity Freeze

Serves: 2

2 bananas, overripe
1 tablespoon applesauce
$1/2$ teaspoon vanilla or almond flavoring

Peel bananas and mash in bowl or food processor. Add applesauce and vanilla or almond flavoring. Cover and place in freezer for several hours. Note: Peaches, pineapple, strawberries, blueberries, etc., can also be added. If using pears or apples, peel and cook in microwave until softened. Core and mash or pureé. Try this with lemon or lime juice.

"This is not Haagen Dazs or Ben & Jerry's, but it's healthy, sweet and frozen!"

Camille Hicks   **Riverton High School, Riverton, UT**

Fruity Tofu Shakes

Serves: 3   250 Cal; 3g Fat; 51g Carbs; 8g Fiber; 8g Protein; 38mg Sodium; 0mg Cholesterol

1 $1/2$ cups fresh or frozen fruit (strawberries, raspberries, peaches, mango, nectarines, pitted cherries)
1 $1/2$ cups orange juice
1 (10.5 ounce) package light tofu, cut up
2 tablespoons honey

Partially thaw the fruit, if frozen. In a blender container, combine fruit, orange juice, tofu and honey. Cover and blend until nearly smooth. Pour into glasses. Makes 3 (1 $1/3$ cup) servings.

"If you've never tried tofu, this thick, fruity breakfast shake is a great start! Soy foods, like tofu, are tops in health benefits providing cancer-fighting and heart-protecting phytochemicals, daidzein and genistein."

Alice Claiborne   **Fairfield High School, Fairfield, CA**

Hot Feta Artichoke Dip

Makes: 2 cups

1 (14 ounce) can artichoke hearts, drained, chopped
2 (4 ounce) packages feta cheese, crumbled
1 cup lowfat mayonnaise
$1/2$ cup Parmesan cheese, shredded
1 clove garlic, minced
Garnish: Chopped tomato, chopped green onions

Preheat oven to 350 degrees. Mix all ingredients together and spoon into a 9" pie plate or an 8" x 8" glass casserole dish. Bake 20 to 25 minuets until lightly browned. Garnish with chopped tomato and green onion, if desired. Serve with assorted whole wheat crackers or pita triangles.

Paula Skrifvars   **Brea Junior High School, Brea, CA**

Judy's Berry Smoothie

Makes: 16 ounces   *Weight Watchers = 5 points*

1 cup mixed berries
1 cup nonfat milk
1 scoop (2 tablespoons) Country Time Lemonade Powder

Place all ingredients in a blender and blend well. Makes a thick, delicious shake!

"The day school was out last year, I joined Weight Watchers. I am not an artificial sugar person so I created this recipe to get me over the sugar cravings! It worked! The lemonade powder gives just the right tang!"

Judy Conner   **Valley High School, Santa Ana, CA**

Kary's Aunt Lisa's Cheese Spread

Makes: 8 ounces

8 ounces regular, lowfat or Neufchatel cream cheese, room temperature
1 cup salad stuffed green olives, well drained
1 tablespoon Worcestershire sauce (or more to taste)
dash garlic powder (optional)

Beat cream cheese to soften. Add green stuffed olives with Worcestershire sauce and beat until well blended. (Olives will break up in the process giving the spread a confetti look.) Add garlic powder, if desired. Refrigerate until serving time. You can shape or mold and decorate to suite the occasion.

"Interesting piquant appetizer served with whole wheat crackers or veggies. Can be made ahead, refrigerated and ready for spontaneous parties or planned events. My dear cousin, Lisa Benson Eichenauer, artist and designer, invented this jazzy stuff and my 18-year old daughter has loved it since she was 4!"

Ellen Black-Eacker   **Nogales High School, La Puente, CA**

Lite Shrimp Spread

Serves: 8 - 10

1 (8 ounce) package light cream cheese
1/2 cup light sour cream
1/4 cup light mayonnaise
1 cup seafood cocktail sauce
2 cups (8 ounces) reduced fat Mozzarella cheese, shredded
2 (4.5 ounce) cans shrimp, rinsed, drained
3 green onions, sliced
3/4 cup tomato, finely chopped

In a bowl, beat cream cheese, sour cream and mayonnaise until smooth. Spread on a large round serving platter and cover with seafood sauce. Sprinkle with remaining ingredients; cover and chill until ready to serve.

*"This colorful and tasty appetizer is always a crowd pleaser.
People will never know you've used lighter ingredients."*

Jan Schulenburg   **Irvine High School, Irvine, CA**

Mac's Olive Hummus

Serves: 14

1 can garbanzo beans, drained, liquid reserved
1 tablespoon cumin seeds, lightly toasted
1 tablespoon olive oil
$1/4$ cup tahini (sesame seed paste)
1 teaspoon onion powder
1 clove garlic, crushed
$1/2$ lemon, juiced
red pepper & black pepper, to taste
1 can black beans, rinsed, drained
paprika
$1/2$ cup pitted Greek olives

Drain garbanzo beans and reserve liquid to add later. Toast cumin seeds in a pan on stove top over medium heat until lightly golden and fragrant. In a food processor fitted with a blade, combine all ingredients except black beans and reserved garbanzo bean liquid. Process until smooth. Add black beans and process until smooth. If it's too thick or dry, add some of the reserved bean liquid. Add additional lemon juice and/or red and black peppers to taste. Chill before serving. Garnish with paprika and Greek olives.

"Serve this healthy dip at a party with pita chips and crudites or as a dip for chicken and grilled salmon. Use as a spread for wraps stuffed with grilled chicken or fish and grilled vegetables. Change the flavors with roasted red bell peppers or fresh herbs or mint leaves."

Holly Pittman   **El Capitan High School, Lakeside, CA**

Mango Smoothie

Serves: 2   *130 Cal; 1g Fat; 3mg Chol.*

1 ripe mango, peeled, pitted, chopped, (about 1 $1/4$ cups)
$3/4$ cup nonfat milk, chilled
$1/4$ cup vanilla nonfat yogurt
$3/4$ teaspoon vanilla
3 ice cubes
pinch salt

Combine all ingredients in blender. Blend until smooth and creamy. Pour into glasses and serve.

"A great way to start the day. Can substitute nectarines or peaches for mango."

Julie Shelburne   **Tulare Union High School, Tulare, CA**

Mango-Ade

Serves: 20

> 2 ripe mangos, peeled, pitted, grated
> 1 3/4 cups white sugar
> 8 cups water, divided
> 1 1/2 cups fresh lemon juice

Peel and shred mango pulp with grater; set aside. In a small saucepan, combine sugar and 1 cup water; bring to a boil and stir to dissolve sugar. Allow to cool to room temperature, then cover and refrigerate until chilled. Remove seeds from lemon juice but leave pulp. In a pitcher, stir together lemon juice and pulp, mango juice and pulp, chilled syrup and remaining water.

> *"This recipe was from a student's family in Mexico. It's an excellent compliment to Latin flavors on a hot summer afternoon."*

Stephanie San Sebastian   **Central High School, Fresno, CA**

Pickled Shrimp

Makes: 2 pounds

> 2 pounds raw shrimp, shelled, deveined
> 3/4 cup olive oil, divided
> 3 cloves garlic, crushed
> 4 (medium) onions, sliced, divided
> 1/2 cup white vinegar
> 1 1/2 teaspoons salt
> 1/4 teaspoon dry mustard
> 1/2 teaspoon pepper
> 2 jalapeño peppers, thinly sliced

Saute shrimp in 1/4 cup olive oil with garlic and 2 sliced onions. Remove from pan and set aside to cool. Combine remaining oil, sliced onions and remaining ingredients to make a sauce. Add shrimp to sauce and marinate in refrigerator at least 24 hours.

> *"At Christmas, I add thinly sliced red bell peppers for color."*

Pat Johnson   **Iron Horse Middle School, San Ramon, CA**

Pineapple Cooler

Serves: 12

    1 half gallon buttermilk
    1 (20 ounce) can crushed pineapple
    juice of 1 lemon
    artificial sweetener, to taste
    ice cubes

Combine all ingredients, except ice, in a large container. Pour desired amount in a blender, add ice and blend until slushy. Taste and adjust sweetener, as desired. Serve.

"Very refreshing. Use lowfat or 1% buttermilk.
My mom made this for us every summer and froze it into sherbet."

April Rosendahl   **Chino High School, Chino, CA**

Portabello and Cheese Bruschetta

Serves: 4   *5 Carbs.*

    1 tablespoon olive oil, divided
    1 teaspoon balsamic vinegar
    1 clove garlic, crushed
    1 (large) portabello mushroom, stems and gills removed
    4 slices low-carb bread
    3 tablespoons ricotta or goat cheese
    1/4 teaspoon salt
    4 tablespoons pesto
    fresh parsley, chopped

Heat oven to 425 degrees. Combine 1 tablespoon oil with vinegar and garlic. Brush on both sides of mushroom. Bake on foil-lined baking sheet 15 to 18 minutes, until golden. Remove from oven, wrap in foil and let stand 5 to 8 minutes to soften. Pat mushroom dry, cut in half, slice thinly crosswise into crescent shapes. Meanwhile, heat broiler. Cut two circles from each bread slice. Broil 4" from broiler, 30 to 40 seconds per side. Mix cheese with salt. Spread each toasted slice with pesto, then with cheese. Top with slightly overlapping mushroom slices. Sprinkle with parsley.

Liz Coleman   **Oroville High School, Oroville, CA**

Spinach-Artichoke Dip

Serves: 8   *177 Cal; 13g Fat; 7.5g Carbs; 2.5g Fiber; 9g Protein*

1 (10 ounce) package spinach, frozen, chopped
1 (13.75 ounce) can artichoke bottoms, thawed, drained
2 cloves garlic
1 (8 ounce) package cream cheese
1 cup Parmesan cheese, grated
1/4 teaspoon pepper

Preheat oven to 350 degrees. Grease a 1 quart ovenproof dish. In a food processor, process spinach, artichokes, garlic, cream cheese, Parmesan and pepper until well combined. Scrape down sides of processor as needed. Spread mixture in prepared dish. Bake about 30 minutes, until warmed through. Serve hot, with cut up vegetables.

"Yummy dip for sports season or any time of year!"

Sonja Tyree   **Ayala High School, Chino Hills, CA**

Spinach-Stuffed Mushrooms

Makes: 20   *32 Cal; 1g Fat*

1 (10 ounce package frozen chopped spinach, thawed
20 (large) fresh mushrooms
nonstick cooking spray
1/3 cup plain fat free yogurt
1/4 cup + 1 tablespoon Parmesan cheese, grated, divided
1/4 cup onion, diced
1/4 cup reduced fat cheddar cheese, shredded
1/4 cup reduced fat Monterey Jack cheese, shredded
1 tablespoon sherry
1/4 teaspoon salt
1/4 teaspoon garlic powder
1/4 teaspoon dried oregano

Preheat broiler. Drain spinach and press between layers of paper towels until barely moist; set aside. Clean mushrooms with damp paper towels. Remove stems and finely chop. Coat a large nonstick skillet with cooking spray; place over medium heat until hot. Add mushroom caps; cook, stirring constantly for 5 minutes; drain. Place caps on rack of broiler pan, stem side up; set aside. Combine spinach, chopped stems, yogurt, 1/4 cup Parmesan cheese, onion, cheeses, sherry, spices and spoon into mushroom caps. Sprinkle with remaining 1 tablespoon Parmesan cheese. Broil 5 minutes or until cheese melts.

"Delicious, impressive appetizer that is low in fat and calories."

Jan Tuttle   **Mills High School, Millbrae, CA**

Tangy Meatballs

Makes: 4 dozen

2 eggs
2 cups oats
1 (12 ounce) can evaporated milk
1 1/2 cups onion, chopped, divided
2 teaspoons salt
1/2 teaspoon pepper
1/2 teaspoon garlic powder
3 pounds lean ground beef
2 cups catsup
1 1/2 cups brown sugar, firmly packed
1 to 2 teaspoons garlic smoke
1/2 teaspoon garlic powder

Preheat oven to 375 degrees. In a large bowl, beat eggs. Add oats, milk, 1 cup chopped onion, salt, pepper and garlic powder. Add the ground beef; mix well. Shape into 1 1/2" balls. Place in two 9" x 13" baking pans. Bake, uncovered at 375 degrees for 30 minutes. Remove from oven and drain. Place meatballs in one pan. In a saucepan, bring remaining ingredients to a boil. Pour over meatballs. Return to oven and bake, uncovered, for 20 minutes.

"A delicious appetizer!"

Vicki Pearl   **Townsend Junior High School, Chino Hills, CA**

Tomato, Basil & Cheese Kabobs

Makes: 20

20 (small) cherry or grape tomatoes
40 (small) fresh basil leaves
20 cherry bocconcini (small balls of fresh Mozzarella cheese)
   or 20 1/2" cubes of Mozzarella cheese

Cut each tomato in half and thread on toothpick, followed by a basil leaf, then a piece of cheese, then another basil leaf and another tomato.

"These are a colorful, healthy and easy appetizer."

Peggy Herndon   **Central Valley High School, Shasta Lake City, CA**

Tropical Sunset Punch

Serves: 16

crushed ice
1 (large) can pineapple juice
1 (2 litre) bottle diet lemon lime soda or ginger ale
2 ounces grenadine syrup

In a clear punch bowl, place crushed ice. Pour pineapple juice over, followed by lemon-lime or ginger ale. Gently drizzle grenadine syrup over punch. As the heavier syrup settles through the punch, it looks like a sunset!

"This is a nice, healthy alternative to overly sweet or alcoholic punches. Use the above proportions to increase as needed."

Pam Bonilla   **Valley View High School, Moreno Valley, CA**

Turkey Wontons
Makes: 4 dozen

1 pound ground turkey
2 green onions, thinly sliced
1 teaspoon garlic salt
dash pepper
1 package won ton wrappers
2 to 4 cups corn oil
cornstarch

Combine ground turkey with green onion and spices; mix well. Place 1 teaspoonful filling in center of each won ton skin. Moisten edges, fold diagonally and seal edges. Press fork tines along sealed edges for decoration. Place on waxed paper covered with a thin layer of cornstarch. Cover with plastic wrap; repeat until all filing is used. In a wok or heavy fry pan, heat 2" oil to 350 degrees. Fry won tons until crisp and golden brown, about 2 to 3 minutes. Drain on paper towels.

"A healthier version, yet still delicious!"

Astrid Curfman   **Newcomb Academy, Long Beach, CA**

Zesty Dressing & Dip
Serves: a crowd

Pace Picante Sauce
Sour Cream

Mix equal amounts of salsa and sour cream. Store in refrigerator at least 1 hour prior to use. Use as a dip for fresh vegetables or as a dressing for your favorite salad. This also makes a great topper for baked potatoes.

"This keeps well in refrigerator. I place it in small containers and bring them to the restaurant with me - saves many calories!"

Georgette Phillips   **Silverado High School, Victorville, CA**

Breads & BAKERY ITEMS

Banana Bread (Low Sugar)

Serves: 24   *140 Cal; 19g Carbs per $3/8$" slice*

$1/2$ cup margarine
$1/2$ cup sugar
3 eggs
2 $3/4$ cup flour, sifted
1 $1/2$ teaspoons baking powder
$1/2$ teaspoon baking soda
1 teaspoon salt
1 $1/2$ cups ripe bananas, mashed (about 3)

Preheat oven to 350 degrees. Cream together margarine and sugar; add eggs and beat well. Sift together dry ingredients. Add to eggs, alternately with banana, mixing well after each addition. Turn into 9" x 5" loaf pan coated with nonstick cooking spray. Bake 50 to 60 minutes or until done. Remove from pan and cool on rack.

Pat Peck   **Folsom High School, Folsom, CA**

Best Bran Muffins

Makes: 5 dozen

2 cups all-bran cereal
2 teaspoons baking soda
2 cups boiling water
1 cup shortening (or $1/2$ cup shortening, $1/2$ cup applesauce)
2 cups sugar
4 eggs
1 quart buttermilk
5 cups flour (may mix white and wheat)
1 tablespoon salt
4 cups bran flake cereal
2 cups dates or raisins
1 cup walnuts, chopped

Stir all-bran cereal and soda into boiling water; set aside to soak. Cream shortening, sugar and eggs. Stir in buttermilk and mix well. Alternate flour and salt with cooled bran mixture, stirring until combined. Fold in bran flakes, fruit and nuts. Store in covered non-metal bowl for up to 6 weeks in refrigerator. To bake, spoon out batter as needed into prepared muffin tins. Bake at 375 degrees for 20 minutes.

"A third generation recipe and now my daughter in college asks me to make the batter so she can take half of it to school. I substitute applesauce for less fat."
Carol Winter   **Hillcrest High School, Midvale, UT**

Bran Flax Muffins

Makes: 15

1 1/2 cups unbleached white flour
3/4 cup flaxseed meal
3/4 cup oat bran
1 cup brown sugar
1 teaspoon baking soda
1 teaspoon baking powder
1/2 teaspoon salt
2 teaspoons cinnamon
1 1/2 cups carrots, shredded
2 apples, peeled, shredded
1/2 cup raisins
1 cup nuts, chopped
3/4 cup milk
2 eggs, beaten
1 teaspoon vanilla

Preheat oven to 350 degrees. Mix together flour, flaxseed meal, oat bran, brown sugar, baking soda, baking powder, salt and cinnamon in a large bowl. Stir in carrots, apples, raisins and nuts. Combine milk, beaten eggs and vanilla. Pour liquid ingredients into dry ingredients and mix just to moist; do not overmix. Fill muffin cups 3/4 full. Bake 15 to 20 minutes.

"This recipe is loaded with foods good for you and they taste like carrot cake."
Rebecca Bolt   **Bear Creek High School, Stockton, CA**

Golden Harvest Muffins

Makes: 36   *204 Cal; 12.8g Fat. (Lowfat version: 91 Cal; .19g Fat)*

      2 cups all purpose flour
      2 cups whole wheat flour
      2 cups sugar
      4 teaspoons baking soda
      4 teaspoons cinnamon
      1 teaspoon salt
      $1/2$ teaspoon cloves
      4 cups (5 medium) apples, peeled, shredded
      1 cup carrots, shredded
      1 cup coconut
      1 cup raisins
      1 cup walnuts or pecans, chopped
      1 $1/2$ cups oil
      $1/2$ cup milk
      4 teaspoons vanilla
      3 eggs, beaten
      Lowfat version:
      Same as above, only omit coconut and nuts, replace oil with applesauce,
      nonfat milk for milk and $3/4$ cup egg beaters for eggs. Reduces calories to
      91 and .19g fat per muffin.

   Preheat oven to 350 degrees. Line 36 muffin cups with paper baking
cups or grease bottoms only. Lightly spoon flour into measuring cup;
level off. In 4 quart bowl, combine all purpose flour, whole wheat flour,
sugar, baking soda, cinnamon, salt and cloves. Add apples, carrots,
coconut, raisins and nuts; mix well. Add oil, milk, vanilla and eggs; stir
just until moistened. Fill lined or greased muffin cups $3/4$ full. Bake 20
to 25 minutes or until toothpick inserted in center comes out clean.
Immediately remove from pan.

   "We made the original recipe and the lowfat version in class.
   Students sampled and judged. Great for student's awareness!"

Phyllis Langlois   **Green Valley High School, Henderson, NV**

Granola

Makes: 12 cups

      1 cup apple juice
      1 cup honey
      1 $1/2$ teaspoons vanilla
      8 cups oatmeal
      1 $1/2$ cups walnuts, chopped
      1 $1/2$ cups raisins
      1 $1/2$ cups dried cranberries

Place apple juice and honey in a glass measuring cup and heat in microwave on HIGH for 4 minutes. Add vanilla and stir. Put oatmeal and nuts in a large mixing bowl and stir in liquid mixture. Let sit 5 minutes to absorb liquid. Bake at 300 degrees for 20 minutes on 2 large, lightly greased jelly roll pans, stirring after 10 minutes. Cereal will be light brown. Place in a large bowl while warm and stir in raisins and cranberries. Cool and place in airtight containers and refrigerate.

"You can add different dried fruits or nuts, to make it your own."

Sue Waterbury   **San Luis Obispo High School, San Luis Obispo, CA**

Healthy Banana Nut Bread

Makes: 2 medium loaves

2 1/2 cups flour
2 teaspoons baking soda
1 teaspoon salt
1 cup applesauce
1 cup Egg Beaters
1 3/4 cup sugar
4 (medium) bananas
1 cup walnuts, chopped

Preheat oven to 350 degrees. Grease and flour two medium-sized loaf pans (use nonstick cooking spray). Combine flour, baking soda and salt in a bowl; set aside. In a larger bowl, combine applesauce, egg substitute and sugar; mix well. Slice bananas into mixture, and continue to mix about 1 minute. Stir in walnuts. Pour into prepared loaf pans. Bake 55 to 60 minutes or until a knife inserted in center comes out clean.

Therese Duffy   **Warren High School, Downey, CA**

Honey Wheat Muffins

Makes: 12

1 cup flour
1 cup whole wheat flour
2 teaspoons baking powder
1/4 teaspoon salt
1 egg
1/2 cup milk
1/2 cup honey
1/4 cup oil

Preheat oven to 400 degrees. Grease muffin pan. In a large bowl, stir together flours, baking powder and salt. In a small bowl, combine egg, milk, honey and oil. Add egg mixture to flour mixture, stirring just enough to moisten. Fill muffin cups $^2/_3$ full. Bake 20 minutes. Remove and serve warm.

Patty Stroming   **Mitchell Senior Elementary, Atwater, CA**

Lemon Blueberry Muffins

Makes: 1 dozen   187 Cal; 4.8g Fat; 32.6g Carbs; 1g Fiber; 3.7g Protein; 264mg Sodium; 30mg Chol

  2 cups all-purpose flour
  $^1/_2$ cup sugar
  1 teaspoon baking powder
  $^1/_2$ teaspoon baking soda
  $^1/_2$ teaspoon salt
  $^1/_8$ teaspoon ground nutmeg
  $^1/_4$ cup butter
  1 $^1/_4$ cups lowfat buttermilk
  1 (large) egg
  1 tablespoons lemon rind, grated
  1 cup blueberries
  nonstick cooking spray
  1 tablespoon fresh lemon juice
  $^1/_2$ cup powdered sugar

Preheat oven to 400 degrees. Lightly spoon flour into dry measuring cups; level with knife. Combine flour and next 5 ingredients in medium bowl; cut in butter with pastry blender or two knives until mixture resembles coarse meal. Combine buttermilk, egg and rind; stir just until moist. Gently fold in blueberries. Spoon batter into 12 muffin cups coated with nonstick cooking spray. Bake 20 minutes or until muffins spring back when lightly touched in center. Remove muffins from pan immediately and place on a wire rack to cool. Combine lemon juice and powdered sugar in small bowl. Drizzle glaze evenly over cooled muffins. Note: You can make these muffins up to 2 days ahead. Glaze just before serving.

"A flavorful recipe that was originally printed in Cooking Light magazine."
Jackie Williams   **Prospect High School, Saratoga, CA**

Low Fat Blueberry Muffins

Makes: 12

  2 cups flour, sifted
  $^1/_2$ cup sugar
  1 tablespoon baking powder
  $^1/_2$ teaspoon salt
  1 egg
  1 cup milk
  $^1/_4$ cup oil
  $^1/_2$ cup blueberries

Preheat oven to 400 degrees. Combine flour, sugar, baking powder and salt in large mixing bowl. Beat egg in small mixing bowl, then add milk and oil. Add liquid ingredients to dry ingredients in the large bowl; stir quickly with fork, until dry ingredients are just moistened. Do not over mix! Batter should be lumpy. Add blueberries and mix gently. Do not overmix, otherwise batter will have a green cast when baked. Spoon batter into muffin cups $2/3$ full. Bake 15 to 20 minutes or until golden brown. Serve hot with butter and/or jelly.

"My students love these. Best right out of the oven.
The best part - only 1 teaspoon of fat and 2 teaspoons sugar per muffin!"
Carol Steele   **La Paz Intermediate School, Mission Viejo, CA**

Lowfat Biscuits

Serves: 12

$1/2$ cup whole wheat flour
1 $1/2$ cups flour
1 tablespoon baking powder
$3/4$ teaspoon salt
$1/2$ teaspoon cream of tartar
3 tablespoons butter, cut into small pieces
$3/4$ cup milk

Preheat oven to 450 degrees. Mix flours, baking powder, salt and cream of tartar in medium bowl. Cut butter into flour mixture until it resembles corn meal. Add milk and stir just until blended together. Turn dough onto lightly floured surface and knead gently for just a few seconds until it comes together. Pat or roll dough to $3/4$" thick. Cut out 12 biscuits and put remaining dough together to get as many biscuits as possible. Place on ungreased cookie sheet. Bake 10 to 13 minutes or until lightly browned.

Jill Burnham   **Bloomington High School, Bloomington, CA**

Lowfat Doughnuts

Makes: 9   *183 Cal; 5.6g Fat; 30g Carbs; 3.2g Protein; 195mg Sodium; 1mg Chol.*

1 $^1/_2$ cups all-purpose flour
$^1/_2$ cup + 1 tablespoon granulated sugar
1 $^1/_2$ teaspoons baking powder
$^1/_4$ teaspoon salt
1 teaspoon ground cinnamon
$^1/_2$ teaspoon ground nutmeg
$^1/_2$ cup 1% lowfat milk
$^1/_4$ cup margarine, melted
$^1/_4$ cup egg substitute
$^1/_2$ teaspoon vanilla
nonstick cooking spray
2 tablespoons powdered sugar

Preheat oven to 400 degrees. Lightly spoon flour into dry measuring cups; level with knife. Combine flour and next 5 ingredients in a large bowl; make a well in center of mixture. Combine milk, margarine, egg substitute and vanilla and stir well with a whisk. Add to flour mixture, stirring just until moistened. Spoon batter by 2 heaping tablespoonfuls into each cup of a mini bundt pan coated with nonstick cooking spray. Smooth tops of batter evenly with knife. Bake 10 minutes or until a wooden pick inserted in center comes out clean. Remove from pan immediately; cool on a wire rack. Repeat with remaining batter. Sift powdered sugar over doughnuts. Serve warm or at room temperature.

Bree Hitchens   **El Modena High School, Orange, CA**

Lowfat Poppy Seed Muffins

Makes: 10

1 cup flour
$^1/_2$ cup sugar
1 tablespoons poppy seed
1 pinch salt
$^1/_4$ teaspoon baking soda
1 teaspoon lemon peel
1 egg
$^1/_2$ teaspoon vanilla
$^1/_2$ cup nonfat lemon yogurt
1 tablespoon butter or margarine, melted
3 tablespoons applesauce

Preheat oven to 400 degrees. Combine flour, sugar, poppy seeds, salt and baking soda and lemon peel. In a separate bowl, mix egg, vanilla, yogurt, melted butter and applesauce. Combine both bowls together and lightly stir. (Batter will be lumpy.) Pour into greased muffin tins and bake 15 minutes.

Gaylene Greenwood   **Roy High School, Roy, UT**

Marvelous Muffins

Makes: 12 muffins

2 cups flour
2 teaspoons baking powder
$1/2$ teaspoon salt
1 cup cranberries, chopped
1 egg, beaten
$1/4$ cup oil
$1/2$ cup molasses
1 $1/2$ cups milk

Preheat oven to 400 degrees. Combine flour, baking powder, salt and cranberries in a bowl. Stir together egg, oil, molasses and milk in another bowl. Combine the mixtures, mixing just until blended. Spoon into a greased or paper-lined muffin tin. Bake 20 to 25 minutes until toothpick inserted in center comes out clean.

"Can also substitute whole wheat flour."

Cheryl Kras   **Saddleback High School, Santa Ana, CA**

Oat & Apricot Breakfast Bars

Makes: 8

1 cup whole wheat flour
1 teaspoon baking powder
$1/2$ cup brown sugar, packed
$1/2$ cup uncooked quick oats
15 dried apricots, diced
2 tablespoons sunflower seeds
1 tablespoon reduced-calorie margarine, melted
$1/2$ cup fat free egg substitute OR 2 eggs

Preheat oven to 350 degrees. Coat an 8" square pan with nonstick cooking spray. Whisk together flour, baking powder, sugar, oats, apricots and sunflower seeds. In another bowl, whisk together margarine and egg substitute. Quicky mix together wet and dry ingredients. Spoon into prepared pan and smooth top. Bake until firm, about 20 minutes. Cool completely before cutting into 8 rectangles.

"These are great to make ahead and freeze for those busy mornings.
The kids make them at school (using regular eggs) and despite seeing whole
wheat and other healthy ingredients on the menu, they like them."

Ruth Anne Schroeder   **River City High School, West Sacramento, CA**

Pumpkin-Carrot Muffins

Makes: 12   *120 Cal; 1g Fat*

$^1/_2$ cup canned pumpkin
$^2/_3$ cup brown sugar
4 egg whites, slightly beaten
$^1/_2$ cup buttermilk
2 teaspoons baking soda
2 teaspoons cinnamon
$^1/_2$ teaspoon salt
3 teaspoons baking powder
1 cup carrots, grated
1 to 1 $^1/_4$ cups whole wheat flour
nonstick cooking spray

Preheat oven to 375 degrees. Mix all ingredients, except flour together; stir in flour just until moistened. Spoon into muffin tins coated with nonstick cooking spray. Bake about 15 minutes.

"For diabetics, replace brown sugar with $^1/_3$ cup each pineapple juice concentrate and apple juice concentrate, increase flour by $^1/_3$ cup."

Linda Stokes   **Riverton High School, Riverton, UT**

Raisin Bran Muffins

Makes: 6 dozen

2 $^1/_2$ cups sugar
5 cups flour
2 tablespoons baking soda
1 teaspoon salt
4 eggs
1 cup applesauce
1 quart buttermilk
1 (15 ounce) box raisin bran cereal

Mix together sugar, flour, baking soda and salt; set aside. Beat eggs in a large bowl. Add applesauce and buttermilk to eggs; stir. Add dry ingredients to liquid ingredients. Fold in cereal. Refrigerate 24 hours. Line muffin tins with paper. Fill $^2/_3$ full and bake at 400 degrees for 15 to 20 minutes until golden brown.

"One of my favorites!"

Maria Montemagni   **Mt. Whitney High School, Visalia, CA**

Refrigerator Bran Muffins

1 cup boiling water
1 cup Nabisco 100% Bran Cereal
$^1/_2$ cup shortening or margarine
1 cup sugar
2 eggs
2 cups buttermilk
2 $^1/_2$ cups flour
2 $^1/_2$ teaspoons baking soda
$^1/_2$ teaspoon salt
2 cups Kellogg's All-Bran Cereal

Preheat oven to 400 degrees. Pour boiling water over Nabisco Bran cereal; set aside. In another bowl, cream shortening and sugar. Blend in eggs and buttermilk and add to bran mixture. Add flour, soda and salt. Stir in Kellogg's All-Bran cereal. Spoon batter into muffin tins and bake 15 to 20 minutes. When a toothpick in center comes out clean, muffins are done. Note: This batter can be stored, covered in refrigerator up to six weeks or used immediately. The recipe can also be easily doubled.

"I received this recipe from my Pastor's wife, Lois Lindley, at my wedding shower 25 years ago. They are delicious. The batter lasts in the refrigerator up to 6 weeks! Bran muffins are always best fresh out of the oven!"
Debbie Farr   **Foothill High School, Santa Ana, CA**

Spiced Pumpkin Bread

Serves: 16   *100 Cal; 1g Fat*

2 cups flour
nonstick cooking spray
1 cup brown sugar
1 tablespoon baking powder
$^1/_4$ teaspoon baking soda
2 teaspoons cinnamon
$^1/_2$ teaspoon nutmeg
$^1/_4$ teaspoon ginger
$^1/_4$ teaspoon cloves
1 (15 ounce) can pumpkin
$^1/_2$ cup skim milk
2 egg whites
$^1/_3$ cup fat free sour cream

Preheat oven to 350 degrees. Spray a bundt pan with cooking spray and set aside. Combine flour, brown sugar, baking powder, baking soda, cinnamon, nutmeg, ginger and cloves in a mixing bowl. In a separate bowl, combine pumpkin, milk, egg whites and sour cream. Stir into dry ingredients just until moistened. Pour batter into prepared bundt pan and bake 60 minutes.

Natalie Henwood   **Riverton High School, Riverton, UT**

Wake-Up Cake

Serves: 6 - 8

$1/3$ cup peanut butter
$1/3$ cup brown sugar
2 $1/2$ tablespoons margarine
1 egg
$1/2$ teaspoon vanilla
1 ripe banana, mashed
$2/3$ cup oats
$1/3$ cup flour
2 tablespoons wheat germ
$1/4$ teaspoon baking soda

Using an electric mixer, beat together peanut butter, brown sugar and margarine. Blend in egg and vanilla. Blend in banana. Stir in oats, flour, wheat germ and baking soda. Mix well until blended. Spread into a greased 9" x 9" pan. Bake at 350 degrees for 20 minutes. Cool and cut into squares.

"This is a good way to get fruit and fiber into teenagers."

LeeAnn Bitner   **Alta High School, Sandy, UT**

Soups & Stews CHILI

Black Bean and Salsa Soup

Serves: 4

1 $1/2$ cups water
2 cubes beef bouillon
2 (15 ounce) cans black beans, drained, rinsed
1 cup thick and chunky salsa
1 teaspoon cumin
4 tablespoons sour cream
2 tablespoons green onion, thinly sliced
tortilla chips

In a 2 quart saucepan, heat water to boiling. Add bouillon and dissolve. Slightly pureé beans in a blender, leaving some chunky. Add beans, salsa and cumin to bouillon. Cook until heated through over low heat. Ladle soup into bowls and place a dollop of sour cream on top; swirl gently. Sprinkle with green onions; add 2 to 3 tortilla chips.

"Amazingly delicious and healthy!"

Anne Hawes   **Cottonwood High School, Salt Lake City, UT**

Canned Cream Soup Substitute

Serves: 9   *76 Cal; 1.33g Fat; 2.66mg Chol.*

2 cups powdered nonfat milk
$3/4$ cup cornstarch
$1/4$ cup instant chicken bouillon
2 tablespoons dried onion flakes
1 teaspoon basil
1 teaspoon thyme
$1/2$ teaspoon pepper

Combine all ingredients, mixing well. Store in air-tight container until ready to use. Equivalent to 9 cans soup. To use: Combine $1/3$ cup dry mix with 1 $1/4$ cups cold water. Cook and stir on stove or in microwave until thickened. Add thickened mixture to casseroles as you would add a can of soup. For example: Add a 4 ounce can of mushrooms, undrained, for cream of mushroom soup. Add $1/2$ cup cooked, diced celery for cream of celery soup. Add 1 cup grated cheddar cheese, $1/2$ cup milk and 1 cup chopped broccoli for cheese broccoli soup. Add 1 cup cooked potato cubes and $1/4$ cup milk for potato soup.

Laurie Giauque   **Olympus High School, Salt Lake City, UT**

Cheddar Chicken Chowder

Serves: 7   306 Cal; 7.5g Fat; 33.7g Carbs; 2.9g Fiber; 25g Protein; 376mg Sodium; 58mg Chol

2 slices bacon
1 pound boneless skinless chicken breasts, cut into bite-sized pieces
1 cup onion, chopped
1 cup red bell pepper, diced
2 cloves garlic, minced
4 $1/2$ cups fat-free, sodium-reduced chicken broth
1 $3/4$ cup red potatoes, peeled, diced
2 $1/4$ cups frozen whole kernel corn
$1/2$ cup all-purpose flour
2 cups 2% lowfat milk
$3/4$ cup cheddar cheese, shredded
$1/2$ teaspoon salt
$1/4$ teaspoon black pepper

Cook bacon in Dutch oven over medium-high heat until crisp. Remove bacon from pan, crumble and set aside. Add chicken, onion, bell pepper and garlic to drippings in pan; saute 5 minutes. Add broth and potato, bring to a boil. Cover, reduce heat and simmer 20 minutes or until potato is tender; add corn. Lightly spoon flour into dry measuring cup and level with knife. Place flour in a bowl. Gradually add milk, stirring with a whisk until blended; add to soup. Bring to a boil over medium-high heat. Reduce to medium heat and simmer 15 minutes or until thick, stirring frequently. Stir in cheddar cheese, salt and pepper. Top with crumbled bacon.

Laurie Owen   **Challenger Middle School, San Diego, CA**

Chicken Soup Parmigiana

Serves: 5 - 6

3 cups water
$1/2$ pound boneless, skinless chicken breasts, cubed
1 (8 ounce) can peeled, diced tomatoes
1 cup zucchini, sliced
1 envelope noodle soup with chicken broth
$1/2$ teaspoon dried oregano
$1/2$ teaspoon garlic powder
$1/3$ cup Mozzarella cheese, shredded
Parmesan cheese, grated

In medium saucepan, combine all ingredients except cheese; bring to a boil and simmer, stirring occasionally, about 5 minutes or until chicken is no longer pink. Spoon into bowls and sprinkle with cheeses.

"A great low-carb, non pasta dish with a chicken parmigiana taste!"

Jeanette Atkinson   **Cheyenne High School, Las Vegas, NV**

Chicken Tortilla Soup

Serves: 4 - 5

nonstick cooking spray
$1/2$ cup onion, chopped
2 tablespoons garlic, minced
16 ounces picante sauce
2 (14 ounce) cans chicken broth
1 (14 ounce) can stewed tomatoes
1 (4 ounce) can diced green chiles
$1/4$ cup cilantro, chopped
1 teaspoon oregano
1 to 2 chicken breasts, cooked, shredded
1 cup Monterey jack cheese, shredded, for garnish
Tortilla chips, reduced fat, crumbled, for garnish

In a 3 quart saucepan, sprayed with nonstick cooking spray, saute onion and garlic. Stir in picante sauce, chicken broth, stewed tomatoes, diced green chiles, cilantro and oregano. Bring to a boil, then add shredded chicken; simmer 20 minutes. Serve soup topped with shredded cheese and crumbled tortilla chips.

"A friend gave me this recipe for a progressive dinner and everybody loved it!
Thanks Kim!"

Shirley Marshman   **West Middle School, Downey, CA**

Chili Turkey with White Beans

3 tablespoons olive oil
2 (medium) onions, chopped
4 cloves garlic, chopped
1 jalapeño, seeded, chopped
2 tablespoons chili powder
2 teaspoons ground cumin
$1/2$ teaspoon salt
$1/2$ teaspoon black pepper
4 cups chicken broth
3 (14.5 ounce) cans diced tomatoes
6 cups turkey, cooked, diced
3 (15.5 ounce) cans cannellini beans, drained, rinsed
Toppings: Grated cheddar cheese; sour cream;
   chopped cilantro; chopped scallions

Heat oil in heavy bottom pan over medium heat. Add onion, garlic, peppers and jalapeño. Cook 5 to 7 minutes or until soft. Add spices, salt and pepper; stir. Add broth and diced tomatoes; bring to a boil. Reduce heat; stir in turkey and beans. Simmer 30 minutes. Serve, with desired toppings.

Shelly Tresley   **McQueen High School, Reno, NV**

Chinese Chicken Noodle Soup

Serves: 4 (2 cups)   *293 Cal; 4g Fat; 35g Carbs; 28g Protein; 650mg Sodium; 34mg Chol.*

2 (3 ounce) packages ramen noodles, broken into 3" lengths
2 teaspoons canola oil
1 tablespoon fresh ginger, grated
2 cloves garlic, minced
3 (15 ounce) cans low-sodium fat free chicken broth
1 tablespoon low-sodium soy sauce
1 teaspoon chili-garlic sauce
2 boneless, skinless chicken breasts, thinly sliced
4 scallions, thinly sliced
2 cups baby spinach

Place noodles (discard seasoning packets) in a large bowl; cover with boiling water and soak 3 minutes. Drain under running water. Divide among four soup bowls. Heat oil over medium heat. Stir fry ginger and garlic about 30 seconds. Add broth, soy sauce, chili-garlic sauce, chicken and pepper, to taste; bring to a simmer (do not boil, as that makes the chicken tough and rubbery). Simmer about 5 minutes.

Remove from heat and stir in scallions and spinach. Ladle over noodles. If desired, you can toss with more chili garlic sauce.

"For a low-carb diet, omit the noodles. Shrimp can be substituted for the chicken. Broccoli, shredded carrots and celery can also be added. Delicious!"
Millie Deeton   **Ayala High School, Chino Hills, CA**

Crab and Asparagus Soup

Serves: 4

> 1 leek, chopped
> 1 whole yellow onion, chopped
> 4 to 5 cloves garlic, chopped
> 1 tablespoon olive oil
> 3 1/4 cups chicken broth
> 1 pound asparagus, cut up
> 1 (8 ounce) can crabmeat, with liquid
> 1 teaspoon sesame oil
> 1 teaspoon soy sauce

In a large saucepan, saute the chopped leek, onion, garlic and olive oil until well softened. Add chicken broth and bring to a boil. Add asparagus and crab meat; simmer 2 to 3 minutes. Stir in sesame oil and soy sauce, mixing thoroughly. Serve warm.

"This is a fast and easy recipe that is low in Carbs, high in Vitamin A and Folic Acid. It's also low in fat and calories."
Donna Abbey   **Pleasant Valley High School, Chico, CA**

Cream of Broccoli Soup

Serves: 4

> 1 cup onion, chopped
> 1 (small) clove garlic, minced
> 2 cups potatoes, diced
> 1/2 cup celery, chopped
> 2 cups water
> 3 cups broccoli florets, chopped
> 1/4 teaspoon thyme
> 1/2 teaspoon basil
> 1/4 teaspoon marjoram
> 1 cup buttermilk
> salt and pepper, to taste
> 1/4 cup Parmesan cheese, grated

In a soup pot, combine onions, garlic, potatoes, celery and water. Bring to a boil, then cover, lower the heat and simmer 20 minutes. Add broccoli and herbs; simmer 10 to 15 minutes until vegetables are tender. Working in batches in a blender, pureé soup with the buttermilk. Return

to soup pot. Add salt and pepper, to taste. Reheat and serve. Sprinkle
with Parmesan cheese.

*"The blending and the buttermilk help to make this a cream soup minus
all the fat. It is also a great way to add fiber to your diet!"*

DeeAnn Verdi   **North Valleys High School, Reno, NV**

Fiesta Soup

Serves: 4

> 1 cup chunky salsa with chipolte
> 1 (15 ounce) can black beans, drained, rinsed
> 1 cup cooked chicken or turkey, diced
> 1 (14.5 ounce) can chicken broth
> 1 cup frozen whole kernel corn
> 1 zucchini, diced
> $1/4$ teaspoon cumin
> $1/4$ teaspoon chili powder
> $1/4$ teaspoon oregano
> *Optional:* Cilantro, sour cream

In a large saucepan, combine all ingredients and bring to a boil over
medium-high heat. Reduce heat and simmer 5 minutes. Garnish with
cilantro and sour cream, if desired.

Cyndi Murdoch   **Orland High School, Orland, CA**

Grandma's Beef Vegetable Soup

Makes: 15 cups

> 1 pound ground beef
> 10 cups water
> 1 $1/2$ cups celery, diced
> 1 cup onion, chopped
> 3 (medium) potatoes, cubed
> 4 carrots, diced (about 2 $1/2$ cups)
> $3/4$ cup dried peas
> $1/2$ cup uncooked rice
> $1/2$ cup pearl barley
> 4 beef bouillon cubes
> 1 quart tomato juice

Brown ground beef; drain. In large saucepan, combine water,
vegetables, peas, rice, barley and bouillon; simmer 1 hour, stirring
occasionally as rice will stick. Stir in cooked ground beef and tomato
juice and simmer 30 minutes longer, stirring so rice doesn't stick.

"Excellent served with fresh bread, bread sticks or crackers."

Cheryl Moyle   **Olympus High School, Salt Lake City, UT**

Hamburger Minestrone

Serves: 6   *320 calories*

> 1 pound ground beef
> 1 (medium) onion, chopped, about $1/2$ cup
> 1 clove garlic, crushed
> 1 $1/4$ cups water
> 1 stalk celery, thinly sliced, about 1 cup
> 1 (small) zucchini, sliced, about 1 cup
> 1 cup cabbage, shredded
> $1/2$ cup uncooked elbow macaroni or broken spaghetti
> 2 teaspoons instant beef bouillon (dry)
> 1 teaspoon Italian seasoning
> $1/2$ teaspoon salt
> 1 (28 ounce) can whole tomatoes, undrained
> 1 (8 ounce) can kidney beans, undrained
> 1 (8 ounce) can whole kernel corn, undrained
> Parmesan cheese, grated

Cook and stir ground beef, onion and garlic in Dutch oven until beef is browned; drain. Stir in remaining ingredients except cheese; break up tomatoes with fork. Heat to boiling; reduce heat; cover and simmer, stirring occasionally, until macaroni is tender, about 15 minutes. Serve hot, topped with grated Parmesan cheese.

"May be cooked down and served as a casserole, if desired."

Phyllis Langlois   **Green Valley High School, Henderson, NV**

Herbed Cucumber Soup with Toasted Almonds

Serves: 4

> $3/4$ cup almonds, chopped, blanched,
> 1 English cucumber, halved, seeded (if necessary)
> 1 $1/2$ cups lowfat plain yogurt
> 1 $1/2$ cups buttermilk
> $1/4$ cup fresh Italian parsley, finely copped
> 2 cloves garlic, minced
> 2 tablespoons chives, finely chopped
> 3 tablespoons fresh dill, finely chopped, divided
> salt and white pepper, freshly ground

Preheat oven to 350 degrees. Spread almonds on a baking sheet and toast until lightly browned and aromatic, 5 to 7 minutes. Coarsely chop half of the cucumber, setting the other half aside. In a food processor, pureé chopped cucumber for about 20 seconds. In a separate bowl, combine yogurt and buttermilk. Stir in pureéd cucumber, parsley, garlic, chives, 2 tablespoons of the dill and $1/2$ cup of the almonds until well combined. Chop the remaining cucumber half into small dice and add it to the soup. Season to taste with salt and white pepper. Cover and

Honey Yogurt Dipping Sauce Page 57

Go-Go Wisconsin Blue Cheese Apple Walnut Salad Page 45

Southwestern Chicken Salad **Page 103**

refrigerate until well chilled, at least 4 hours. Taste and adjust seasoning again just before serving. Ladle into chilled bowls and garnish with remaining 2 tablespoons toasted almonds and remaining 1 tablespoon chopped dill. Serve immediately. Note: When toasting almonds, remove them from oven a shade lighter than you desire as they will continue to toast even after removing from oven.

"Good calcium source low in fat and calories and high in flavor!"

Donna Abbey   **Pleasant Valley High School, Chico, CA**

Italian Potato Soup

Serves: 6 - 8

> 3 (large) hot Italian sausage links
> 3 slices bacon, chopped
> 1 (medium) onion, chopped
> 2 cloves garlic, minced
> 10 cups water
> 10 chicken bouillon cubes
> 3 cups cauliflower, sliced or chopped
> 3 cups Kale, chopped
> 3/4 cup heavy cream

Preheat oven to 450 degrees. Bake sausage links in oven for about 30 minutes. Remove from oven, slice lengthwise, then slice into small pieces; set aside. Fry bacon in a large pot. When bacon is almost done, add onion, sauteing until golden. Add garlic and saute 1 minute. Add water, bouillon and cauliflower and simmer for about 20 minutes. Stir sausage into soup. Stir in kale and heavy cream and simmer about 5 minutes more.

"Adapted from the Olive Garden potato soup recipe, one of my favorites!"

Cari Sheridan   **Grace Yokley Middle School, Ontario, CA**

Low Calorie Vegetable Soup

Serves: 6

> 1 1/2 pounds lean ground beef
> 1 (small) cabbage, sliced
> 6 carrots, thinly sliced
> 1 onion, chopped
> 1 green pepper, chopped
> 2 to 3 cups celery, sliced
> 1 teaspoon sugar (optional)
> 1 (large) can tomato juice
> 2 cups water
> salt and pepper, to taste
> Italian seasoning, to taste

Brown ground beef; drain excess grease. Add remaining ingredients and simmer until vegetables are tender, about 20 minutes. Adjust seasonings if necessary. Note: Ground beef can be refrigerated several hours or overnight, after cooking, to remove as much fat as possible.

"Easy to make as well as low calorie."

Lindy Cooper   **Simi Valley High School, Simi Valley, CA**

Lowfat Mexican Soup

Serves: 4   *Weight Watchers 1 = 1 point*

  2 cans chicken or beef broth
  1 can chili beans
  1 can black beans
  1 can corn
  1 can 99% Fat Free Chili (Turkey or Beef)
  1 can Mexican stewed tomatoes
  1 cup mild salsa
  Toppings: fat free sour cream; fat free grated cheese; lowfat tortilla chips;
     chopped green onions; chopped cilantro

Mix ingredients together; simmer 5 minutes. Serve topped with desired toppings.

"This low calorie soup is delicious.
A 1 cup serving counts as 1 point on Weight Watchers."

Lura Staffanson   **Centennial High School, Corona, CA**

Luscious Lentil Soup

Serves: 8

  2 tablespoons olive oil
  2 cups onion, chopped
  4 carrots, coarsely grated
  1 teaspoon marjoram, crumbled
  1 teaspoon thyme, crumbled
  1 (28 ounce) can tomatoes with juice, coarsely chopped
  7 cups broth (beef, chicken or vegetable)
  1 1/2 cups dried lentils, rinsed
  salt and pepper, to taste
  6 ounces dry red wine
  1/3 cup fresh parsley, chopped
  4 ounces cheddar cheese, grated

Heat oil in large sauce pot and saute onion, carrots, marjoram and thyme, stirring the vegetables for 5 minutes. Add tomatoes with juice, broth and lentils. Bring soup to a boil, reduce heat, cover pan and simmer about 1 hour or until lentils are tender. Add salt, pepper, wine and parsley and simmer a few minutes more. Serve with cheese sprinkled on top.

"This recipe is very good, very healthy and easy to freeze."

Marilyn Bankhead　　　　　　　　**San Marcos High School, San Marcos, CA**

Sassy Black Bean Soup

Serves: 6　　　　　　　　　　　　　　*129 Calories per 1 cup serving*

1 tablespoon olive oil
1 cup onion, chopped
2 (small) cloves garlic, minced
2 (15 ounce) cans black beans, drained
1 (14.5 ounce) can no salt added stewed tomatoes, undrained, chopped
1 (10.5 ounce) can low sodium chicken broth
$1/2$ cup picante sauce
$1/4$ cup water
1 teaspoon ground cumin
2 tablespoons fresh lime juice
cilantro, freshly chopped

Heat oil in large nonstick saucepan over medium heat until hot. Add onion and garlic; saute until tender. Do not burn. Add black beans and next 5 ingredients; stir well. Bring to a boil, reduce heat and simmer, uncovered, 15 minutes. Remove from heat stir in lime juice. Serve, topped with chopped cilantro.

"A quick, spicy, healthy soup that tastes fresh and adds a little zip to a meal!"

Jackie Williams　　　　　　　　**Prospect High School, Saratoga, CA**

Shrimp Corn Chowder

Makes: 7 cups

1 tablespoon butter
$1/4$ cup green onions, chopped
1 clove garlic, minced
$1/8$ teaspoon cayenne pepper
1 (3 ounce) package cream cheese, softened, cubed
2 cans 98% fat free Campbell's Cream of Potato Soup
1 $1/2$ soup cans 1% lowfat milk
2 cups frozen shrimp, cleaned, thawed
1 (10 ounce) can corn, undrained

In large saucepan, melt butter, then add green onions, garlic and pepper; saute until tender. Blend in cream cheese, soup and milk. Stir until cream cheese is melted. Add shrimp and corn and bring to a boil; reduce heat, cover and simmer 10 minutes. Serve hot.

"Most ingredients are easy to keep in your freezer and pantry. Lowfat soup, cheese and milk can be used, it still tastes delicious. A meal in itself."

Mary Jo Cali　　　　　　　　**Arroyo Grande High School, Arroyo Grande, CA**

Shrimp Creole Stew

Serves: 4   *131 Cal; 1g Fat; 9g Carbs; 20g Protein*

1 1/2 cups (small) raw shrimp, cleaned, shelled, deveined
1 (16 ounce) bag frozen broccoli/cauliflower/red pepper blend
1 (14.5 ounce) can diced tomatoes, with juice
1 teaspoon hot pepper sauce
1 teaspoon vegetable oil

In large saucepan, combine all ingredients. Cover and bring to a boil. Reduce heat to medium-low; simmer 20 minutes or until shrimp turn opaque.

"Quick, easy and tasty!"

Wendy Duncan   **West Covina High School, West Covina, CA**

Stracciatella (Italian Wedding Soup)

Serves: 4 - 6

3 1/2 cups chicken broth (homemade or canned)
1 pound fresh spinach, washed, trimmed, chopped
1 egg
1/2 cup Parmesan cheese, grated
1 tablespoon flour
salt and pepper, to taste

Bring 1 cup of the broth to a boil; add spinach and cook until softened but still bright green. Remove spinach with a slotted spoon and set aside. Add remaining broth to pot and bring to a boil. Meanwhile, beat egg lightly with a fork. Beat in 1/4 cup of the cheese and flour. When broth boils, pour in egg mixture, stirring constantly for a few seconds until it cooks into rags. Add reserved spinach, salt and pepper. Serve immediately, passing additional grated cheese.

"This recipe was inspired by a wonderful restaurant in Visalia, CA. Once I figured this simple mixture out, all my lunch lady group had to have this recipe! Simple, fresh and healthy! High in beta carotene, Vitamin K, A and Potassium!"

Stephanie San Sebastian   **Central High School, Fresno, CA**

Tortilla Soup

Serves: 4

1 tablespoon oil (optional)
1 onion, thinly sliced
2 cloves garlic, minced
1 cup canned whole tomatoes, drained
1 teaspoon cumin
salt and pepper, to taste
4 cups chicken broth
1 to 2 chicken breasts, boneless, skinless, cut into small chunks
Optional: Sliced avocado, grated pepper jack cheese,
    crisply fried tortilla strips

Using a nonstick pan heat oil, if using, and saute onions and garlic until golden, about 10 minutes. Blend tomatoes and onion/garlic mixture in blender until smooth. Return to pan, add cumin, season with salt and pepper and cook 10 minutes, stirring often. Put chicken broth and tomato mixture in large saucepan and cook 20 minutes, partially covered. Add cut up chicken and cook 3 to 5 minutes, until cooked. To serve: Place avocado slices in bowls, add soup and top with cheese and fried tortilla strips. You may also use shrimp instead of chicken. To lower calories, omit optional items.

"A delicious versatile, easy winter soup.
Make the basic tomato soup and have fun with meats and toppings."

Beth Leighton   **Helix Charter High School, La Mesa, CA**

Turkey Taco Soup

Serves: 6 - 8

nonstick cooking spray
1 (medium) onion, diced
$1/2$ pound ground turkey
1 package taco seasoning mix
1 package Ranch dressing mix
3 (15 ounce) cans Mexican chili beans (no meat)
1 (4.5 ounce) can diced green chiles
1 (16 ounce) can corn, drained
1 $1/2$ cups water
1 (15 ounce) can diced tomatoes

Spray a skillet with nonstick cooking spray. Saute onions until translucent, then add ground turkey and continue cooking until done. Add remaining ingredients and stir well. Cook until heated through. Serve hot.

"You can freeze in 1-cup servings in plastic freezer bags. Thaw and heat."

Jennifer Hill   **Kearns High School, Kearns, UT**

Salads Slaws & DRESSINGS

24-Hour Fruit Salad

Serves: 6 - 8

2 (large) cans fruit cocktail, drained
2 cans Mandarin oranges, drained
2 bananas, peeled, sliced
1 to 2 cups light whipped topping
Optional: Additional fresh or canned fruit;
$^1/_2$ cup miniature marshmallows

Drain juices from all canned fruits. Mix all ingredients together, including optional items, if using, except bananas. Refrigerate overnight. Just before serving, add sliced bananas.

Bonnie Landin Garden Grove High School, Garden Grove, CA

Apple Cole Slaw

Serves: 12 *4g Fat; 11g Carbs; 1g Protein; 5mg Chol.*

$^1/_2$ head green cabbage, shredded
2 (medium) red apples, diced
$^1/_2$ cup green onion
1 green pepper, thinly sliced
$^1/_4$ cup sugar + $^1/_4$ teaspoon sugar, divided
$^1/_2$ teaspoon seasoned salt
$^1/_4$ teaspoon pepper
1 cup light mayonnaise
$^1/_3$ cup vinegar

In large bowl, toss together cabbage, apples, green onion and green pepper. Sprinkle with $^1/_4$ teaspoon sugar, salt and pepper. In a separate bowl, combine mayonnaise, $^1/_4$ cup sugar and vinegar. Pour over cabbage mixture and toss lightly. Chill. Eat up!

Daphne Stockdale Riverton High School, Riverton, UT

Autumn Salad

Serves: 8

Glazed Pecans:
$^1/_4$ cup butter
$^1/_4$ cup light corn syrup
2 tablespoons water
1 teaspoon salt
1 pound pecans, shelled
Salad:
1 head red lettuce
1 head Bibb lettuce
2 Red Delicious apples
$^3/_4$ cup goat cheese, crumbled
Dressing:
$^1/_2$ cup walnut oil
$^1/_4$ cup cider vinegar
2 tablespoons shallot, minced
2 tablespoons lemon juice
1 tablespoon pure maple syrup
$^1/_4$ teaspoon salt
$^1/_4$ teaspoon fresh pepper

Line a baking sheet with foil. Combine butter, corn syrup, water and salt in a saucepan. Bring to a boil, add pecans and stir to completely coat nuts. Spread nuts onto baking sheet and bake at 250 degrees for 1 hour, stirring every 10 minutes. Use $^3/_4$ cup nuts for recipe; store remaining pecans in an air-tight container. To assemble salad, tear lettuce into bite-sized pieces. Cut apples into thin wedges. Toss together with goat cheese and glazed pecans. Stir together dressing ingredients and pour over salad; toss to coat.

*"Delicious salad made with apples, strawberries,
pears or even red flame grapes. Enjoy!"*

Adriana Molinaro   **Granite Hills High School, El Cajon, CA**

Caribbean Potato Salad

Serves: 4 ($^1/_2$ cup)   *109 Cal; 5.4g Fat; 2.9g Fiber Weight Watchers = 2 points*

1 (medium) red or white potato, cut into $^1/_2$" cubes
1 $^1/_2$ tablespoons canola oil
1 $^1/_2$ tablespoons fresh lime juice
1 teaspoon chili powder
$^1/_4$ teaspoon salt
$^1/_8$ teaspoon hot pepper sauce, to taste
$^1/_2$ cup black beans, drained, rinsed
$^1/_3$ cup frozen corn kernels, thawed
$^1/_3$ cup tomato, diced
3 tablespoons green onion, sliced

In a small saucepan, cook potato, covered in 2" of boiling water, until tender, about 10 minutes. Drain and cool. Meanwhile, prepare dressing in medium bowl. Whisk together oil, lime juice, chili powder, salt and hot sauce. Add cooled potatoes, beans, corn, tomato and green onions and toss gently. Serve immediately or refrigerate, covered, until chilled.

"I have recently learned how to eat healthier. This new Weight Watcher recipe from the Potato Board makes traditional potato salad seem boring!"

Shirley Blough   **Hillside Middle School, Simi Valley, CA**

Cheese & Peas Salad

Serves: 4 - 6

    1 cup mayonnaise
    1 tablespoon sugar
    $1/2$ teaspoon salt
    1 cup celery, thinly sliced
    1 to 2 green onions, minced
    1 (10 ounce) package frozen peas
    1 can water chestnuts, well drained
    $1/2$ pound Monterey Jack cheese, diced into $1/2$" cubes
    2 cups head lettuce, torn into bite sized pieces.

Mix together mayonnaise, sugar and salt. In serving bowl, combine celery, green onion, peas and water chestnuts; toss with dressing. Just before serving, toss salad with cheese and lettuce.

"A refreshing salad. People often ask for the recipe!"

Barbara Henshaw   **Foothill High School, Pleasanton, CA**

Chicken Cabbage Salad

Serves: 8

    1 head cabbage, shredded
    2 bunches green onion, chopped
    2 cups chicken, cubed
    2 packages ramen noodles, uncooked, broken into pieces
    $1/4$ cup almonds, sliced
    3 tablespoons sesame seeds
    nonstick cooking spray
    4 tablespoons sugar
    $1/4$ cup tarragon vinegar
    $1/4$ cup olive oil
    $1/2$ teaspoon pepper
    2 tablespoons soy sauce
    2 seasoning packets from ramen noodles

Place cabbage in large serving bowl. Toss with green onion, cooked chicken and noodles. Spray a fry pan with nonstick cooking spray. Place almonds and sesame seeds in pan and toast over medium heat until browned; cool. Add to cabbage mixture. Combine sugar, vinegar, oil, pepper, soy sauce and seasoning packets. Pour over cabbage mixture and toss to coat. Add almonds, sesame seeds and toss again; serve.

"Best cabbage salad ever - my students love it!"

Kelly Smith   **Las Vegas High School Las Vegas, NV**

Chicken Salad

Serves: 6

4 boneless, skinless chicken breasts
2 green onions, chopped
$1/2$ cup cashews, chopped
2 stalks celery, chopped
1 teaspoon celery seed
$3/4$ cup lowfat mayonnaise
1 tablespoon Dijon mustard
salt and pepper, to taste

Microwave or boil chicken breasts until done. Chop into bite-sized pieces. Mix with remaining ingredients.

"This can be served on bed of butter lettuce as a side dish or on bread for a sandwich."

Deanna Lee   **Marina High School, Huntington Beach, CA**

Chicken Salad

Serves: 8

3 (large) apples, peeled, cored, diced
1 tablespoon orange or apple juice concentrate
4 chicken breasts, cooked, deboned, chopped
5 stalks celery, diced
$1/4$ cup mayonnaise (optional)
$1/2$ cup ranch dressing

Toss diced apples with juice concentrate to prevent browning. Place chicken, apples and celery in a large bowl. Toss with mayonnaise and dressing. *Serving Suggestions:* Serve on a bed of dark, fresh greens, such as kale, spinach or red leaf; in a sliced, open tomato on a bed of lettuce; on whole wheat bread or croissant for sandwich; in a low-carb wrap; in a puff pastry or cream puff shell as an appetizer.

"If you are using organically grown apples, keep the peel; contains a large concentration of nutrients just under the skin. Popular at summer parties."

Christine Becker   **Paradise Intermediate School, Paradise, CA**

Chilled Asparagus Dijon Salad

Serves: 6   *120 Cal; 7g Fat; 300mg Sodium; 2mg Cholesterol*

  1 (8 ounce) package light cream cheese
  2 tablespoons lemon juice
  2 tablespoons nonfat milk
  1 tablespoon Dijon mustard
  1 1/2 pounds asparagus spears, cooked, chilled

Place all ingredients, except asparagus, in blender or food processor container; cover. Blend until smooth. Cover; refrigerate. Arrange asparagus on individual salad plates; pour dressing over asparagus. Garnish with lemon peel, if desired.

Kathie Baczynski   **Mt. Carmel High School, Poway, CA**

Confetti Salad

Serves: 6   *196 Cal; 11g Fat; 19g Carbs; 5g Fiber; 6g Protein; 118mg Sodium*

  2 cups red cabbage, shredded
  1 (19 ounce) can white (cannellini) beans, drained and rinsed
  1 (11 ounce) can Mandarin oranges, drained
  1/3 cup walnuts, toasted
  2 (large) scallions, sliced
  3 tablespoons extra virgin olive oil
  2 tablespoons balsamic vinegar
  2 tablespoons orange juice
  salt and pepper, to taste

Put first 5 ingredients in a bowl. In another bowl, whisk together oil, vinegar and juice; salt and pepper to taste, Toss with salad and serve.

"This colorful, crispy salad is delicious and goes great with broiled fish."

Carole Delap   **Golden West High School, Visalia, CA**

Cranberry Jello Salad

Serves: 9

  1 package black cherry jello
  1 package cranberries, frozen
  1/2 cup pineapple, chopped
  1/2 to 3/4 cup pecans, chopped
  Best Foods (Hellman's) mayonnaise for topping

Prepare jello as directed on box using in 8" square pan. When it starts to jell, add remaining ingredients. Chill until thoroughly set. Serve on lettuce leaf and top with mayonnaise.

"If possible, buy frozen cranberries with orange.
Otherwise, some orange zest adds a nice flavor."

Gayle Grigg   **Hendrix Junior High School, Chandler, AZ**

Cranberry Nut Salad

Serves: 8 - 10   *1076 Cal; 109g Fat; 29g Carb.*

1 cup pecans
sugar, to taste
2 heads lettuce (red, curly, romaine or butter)
$1/2$ cup dried cranberries
1 cup gala apple or any crisp flavorful apple, diced
Dressing:
3 tablespoons cider vinegar
$1/2$ cup salad oil
2 tablespoons sugar
$1/2$ teaspoon salt
$1/2$ teaspoon dry mustard
$1/2$ teaspoon onion powder

Cover pecans with water for one minute. Drain immediately and place
in bowl; lightly spoon sugar over top. Remove excess sugar, place
pecans on greased cookie sheet and bake at 375 degrees for
approximately 10 minutes or until lightly browned. Remove from oven
and cool. Rinse and dry lettuce, tear into pieces and place in large bowl.
Add cranberries, apples and cooled pecans. Using a jar with tight-fitting
lid, combine dressing ingredients and shake until combined. When ready
to serve, toss lightly with salad dressing, using only amount needed to
make lettuce shine.

Sonja Erickson   **Maria Carrillo High School, Santa Rosa, CA**

Crisp Spinach Salad

Serves: 4 - 6

1 $1/2$ pounds fresh spinach
8 ounces fresh bean sprouts
1 (5 or 6 ounce) cans water chestnuts, drained
5 slices bacon
$2/3$ cup salad oil
$1/3$ cup sugar
$1/3$ cup ketchup
$1/3$ cup red wine vinegar
$1/3$ cup onion, finely chopped
2 teaspoons Worcestershire sauce
salt and pepper, to taste
2 hard-cooked eggs, peeled, sliced

Trim and discard tough spinach stems; rinse leaves well and pat dry.
Break into bite-sized pieces. In a large bowl, combine spinach, bean
sprouts and water chestnuts. In a frying pan, fry bacon until crisp; drain
and crumble and add to spinach. Cover and refrigerate. In a small bowl,
combine oil, sugar, ketchup, vinegar, onion and Worcestershire sauce;

shake or stir until well combined. Cover and chill. Just before serving, pour dressing over spinach and toss gently until well mixed. Garnish with sliced eggs.

"Very impressive! Great with an elegant dinner."

Sharron Maurice   **Blythe Middle School, Blythe, CA**

Cucumbers in Yogurt

Serves: 6

> 2 cucumbers, peeled, thinly sliced
> 3 tablespoons fresh parsley, chopped
> 1 tablespoon dried dill or 3 tablespoons fresh dill, chopped
> 1 1/2 cups plain yogurt
> 2 to 3 tablespoons fresh lemon juice
> 1 tablespoon olive oil
> 3 cloves garlic, pressed
> 1 teaspoon freshly ground pepper
> 3/4 teaspoon salt

Toss together and chill.

"A wonderful, refreshing side salad served with barbecued chicken and ribs!"

Sue Campbell   **Marsh Junior High School, Chico, CA**

Fruit & Yogurt Salad

Serves: 4

> 1 apple, cored, cut into pieces
> 1 banana, peeled, sliced
> 1 orange, peeled, cut into pieces
> 1/4 cup raisins
> 2 tablespoons lemon juice
> 4 lettuce leaves
> 1/4 cup yogurt

Combine fruit with lemon juice and toss well. Place lettuce leaves on small plates. Place a scoop of fruit on top of each leaf. Top each with spoonful of yogurt and serve.

Patty Stroming   **Mitchell Senior Elementary, Atwater, CA**

Fruited Chicken Salad

Serves: 6

> 1 orange, peeled, diced
> 1 bunch Thompson seedless grapes
> 1 apple, diced
> 1 banana, peeled, sliced
> 2 tablespoons almonds, sliced
> 3 cups chicken breast, broiled or roasted, cubed
> 1 cup lowfat mayonnaise
> lettuce leaves

Mix prepared fruit in large bowl with almonds and cubed chicken. Stir in mayonnaise. Chill. Serve on lettuce leaves.

"Great for summer - refreshing!"

Pat Smith   **Kern Valley High School, Lake Isabella, CA**

Go-Go Wisconsin Blue Cheese Apple Walnut Salad

Serves: 2 - 4

Photo opposite page 32

> $1/2$ cup walnut pieces
> 1 package salad greens, chilled
> 2 (large) red apples (Braeburn, Gala. Fiji, Delicious), washed, dried
> 4 ounces Wisconsin Feta or Wisconsin Blue Cheese, crumbled
> 1 cup bottled honey Dijon dressing

Heat oven to 350 degrees. Spread walnut pieces in a single layer on a baking sheet and bake 8 to 10 minutes until they begin to smell fragrant. Remove to paper plate to cool. Meanwhile, divide the chilled salad greens evenly on 4 chilled plates. Core, slice and chop apples into $1/2$" pieces. Divide and sprinkle evenly over top of salad greens. Sprinkle crumbled cheese and cooled walnuts evenly over apples. Drizzle each salad with dressing.

Wisconsin Milk Marketing Board, Inc.   **Madison, WI**

Greek Salad - Village Style

Serves: 4

$^1/_2$ head romaine lettuce, washed, torn into bite-sized pieces
$^1/_2$ (large) bell pepper, sliced
$^1/_2$ cucumber, thinly sliced
$^1/_4$ red onion, thinly sliced
2 (medium) tomatoes, sliced
3 ounces Feta cheese, crumbled
Greek (Kalamata) olives, pitted
Dressing:
juice from 1 lemon
olive oil to equal lemon juice
1 clove garlic, crushed
2 teaspoons dried oregano

Prepare salad in large bowl, reserving Feta cheese and olives for last. In a small bowl, combine dressing ingredients. Beat with a fork or wire whisk. Pour over salad and toss until well coated. Garnish with olives and crumbled Feta cheese.

"This recipe, which my sister got from her Greek mother-in-law over ten years ago, is very similar to the one Dr. Agatston has in his book, The South Beach Diet. *Great for lunch, topped with cooked, sliced chicken breast or meat."*
Ellen Gordon   **Colton High School, Colton, CA**

Greek Salad with Lemon Dressing

Serves: 8   *130 Cal; 11g Fat; 7g Carbs.; 2g Fiber; 3g Protein; 320mg Sodium; 10mg Chol.*

Salad:
7 ounces spinach, torn into bite-sized pieces to make 5 cups
1 head Boston lettuce, torn into bite-sized pieces to make 4 cups
$^1/_2$ cup feta cheese, crumbled
$^1/_4$ cup green onion, sliced
24 pitted, ripe olives
3 (medium) tomatoes, cut into wedges
1 (medium) cucumber, sliced
Dressing:
$^1/_4$ cup vegetable oil
2 tablespoons lemon juice
$^1/_2$ teaspoon sugar
1 $^1/_2$ teaspoons Dijon mustard
$^1/_4$ teaspoon salt
$^1/_8$ teaspoon pepper

Combine salad ingredients together in large salad bowl; set aside. Using tightly covered container, combine dressing ingredients and shake well. Toss dressing with salad and serve.

"This recipe won first place in both Regional and State FHA competitions in 1988!"

Rita Urquidi   **Nogales High School, La Puente, CA**

Green Salad with Orange Dressing

Serves: 4

Lettuce, any combination of different types
red onion, sliced
Dressing:
$1/3$ cup orange juice (fresh is best)
$1/2$ teaspoon orange peel, grated
2 tablespoons red wine vinegar
$1/2$ cup olive or vegetable oil
1 tablespoon dry Good Seasons Italian Dressing Mix
1 tablespoon sugar
Optional: Canned pears, cut; Mandarin orange slices;
    caramelized almonds; water chestnuts, sliced

Toss lettuce and onion together in large salad bowl. Combine dressing ingredients in a blender and mix well. Pour desired amount over salad greens and toss well. Add optional items, if desired.

"This is one of my favorite salad dressings.
It works well on any type of lettuce and combination of green salad."

Camille Hicks   **Riverton High School, Riverton, UT**

Jalapeño Dressing

Serves: 4 - 6

2 tablespoons cilantro, chopped
2 tablespoons lime juice
1 (small) jalapeño chile, seeded, finely chopped
2 teaspoons sugar
1 tablespoon oil
assorted fresh fruit

Mix first six ingredients. Toss dressing with assorted fresh fruit.

"This makes a tangy salad that goes well with a summer BBQ."

Venetta Ramm   **La Habra High School, La Habra, CA**

Jicama & Carrot Salad

Serves: 6   *99 Cal; 6.7g Fat; 8.8g Carbs; 2.6g Fiber; 2.9g Protein*

2 tomatoes, diced
$1/_2$ (large) jicama, peeled, sliced match stick style
2 carrots, sliced match stick style
2 stalks bok choy, chopped
Dressing:
$1/_3$ cup lime juice, freshly squeezed
$1/_4$ cup apple juice
1 teaspoon chili powder
1 teaspoon salt
2 shallots, minced
2 tablespoons Dijon mustard
$1/_3$ cup olive oil
radish roses (optional)

Toss together tomatoes, jicama, carrots and bok choy. In separate bowl, whisk together dressing ingredients thoroughly. Pour dressing over salad ingredients and toss well. Garnish with radish roses, if desired.

Lori Luna   **Lemoore High School, Lemoore, CA**

Jicama, Orange & Cilantro Salad

Serves: 4   *38 Cal; 9g Carbs; 4g Fiber; 1g Protein; 4mg Sodium;*

8 navel oranges, peeled
12 ounces jicama, peeled, cut into 2" x $1/_2$" x $1/_4$" sticks
$1/_2$ (small) red onion, thinly sliced, lengthwise
$1/_4$ cup cilantro leaves, minced
1 tablespoon fresh lemon juice, or to taste
$3/_4$ teaspoon salt, or to taste
40 pine nuts (2 slightly rounded teaspoons), toasted until golden

Remove pith from orange with serrated knife and cut sections free from membranes; reserve juice. Combine with remaining ingredients, except pine nuts, and toss gently. Just before serving, sprinkle with toasted pine nuts. Note: Salad may be made up to 1 day ahead. Cover and chill in refrigerator until ready to serve.

Sonja Erickson   **Maria Carrillo High School, Santa Rosa, CA**

Lowfat Jello Pretzel Salad

Serves: 12

2 cups pretzels, crushed
$1/2$ cup butter, melted
3 tablespoons +1 cup sugar, divided
8 ounces fat free cream cheese
8 ounces fat free Cool Whip
1 (large) package raspberry jello
1 cup boiling water
2 cups cold water
2 to 3 cups raspberries

Mix pretzels, butter and 3 tablespoons sugar together. Press into 9" x 13" pan. Bake at 350 degrees for 7 minutes; cool. Cream together cream cheese and 1 cup sugar. Fold in Cool Whip. Spread over pretzels. Dissolve jello in boiling water; stir in cold water and raspberries. Pour over cheese layer, Chill until set.

"A family favorite salad - made lowfat!"

Jeanette Atkinson   **Cheyenne High School, Las Vegas, NV**

Lowfat Macaroni Salad

Serves: 12

4 $1/2$ cups macaroni, cooked
$3/4$ cup reduced fat mayonnaise
$1/4$ cup fat free sour cream
3 tablespoons sweet pickle relish
1 (medium) green pepper, seeded, diced
1 (medium) carrot, diced
$1/4$ cup red onion, minced
$1/8$ teaspoon salt, or to taste
$1/8$ teaspoon black pepper, or to taste

While macaroni is still warm, add mayonnaise, sour cream and relish; toss to coat. Add peppers, carrot and onion; toss to combine. Season to taste with salt and pepper. Serve warm or chilled.

"My family loves this (mother-in-law approved!). I like its color also.
A lot livelier and a delicious lowfat substitute for the traditional version."

Ruth Anne Schroeder   **River City High School, West Sacramento, CA**

Mandarin Raspberry Salad

Serves: 6   *100 Cal; 7g Fat; 8 Carbs; 3g Protein; 104mg Sodium*

$^1/_2$ cup raspberry juice (may substitute cranberry juice)
3 tablespoons cider vinegar
1 tablespoon olive oil
1 (8 ounce) package Spring Salad Mix
2 (11 ounce) cans Mandarin oranges, drained
$^1/_4$ cup pecans, toasted
$^1/_2$ cup Monterey jack cheese, grated

In a small jar or mixing bowl, mix together juice, vinegar and olive oil; refrigerate. In a salad bowl, mix together salad mix, oranges and pecans. Toss with salad dressing. Sprinkle cheese on top.

"Add grilled chicken slices to make an entree."

Dotti Jones   **Etiwanda High School, Rancho Cucamonga, CA**

Mango Raspberry Salad

Serves: 4   *100 Cal; 8g Fat; 4g Carbs; 3g Protein*

3 to 4 cups lettuce greens
1 cup mango, peeled, diced
1 cup fresh raspberries
$^1/_4$ cup Gorgonzola cheese
1 tablespoon olive oil
1 tablespoon water
1 tablespoon raspberry vinegar
dash salt and pepper

Combine assorted lettuce greens in medium salad bowl. Add mango, raspberries and cheese. Shake remaining ingredients in a small jar and pour over salad. Toss to coat and serve immediately.

"Salad dressing can be doubled if more is desired."

Marie Coots   **Huntington Beach High School, Huntington Beach, CA**

Oriental Cabbage Salad

Serves: 4   *103 Cal; 9g Fat; 5g Carbs; 2g Fiber;2g Protein; 15mg Sodium*

$^1/_2$ (small) head green cabbage, shredded
3 scallions, chopped
2 tablespoons dark sesame oil
2 tablespoons rice wine vinegar
2 tablespoons sesame seeds, toasted

Combine cabbage, scallions, oil and vinegar; toss well and chill until ready to serve. Add sesame seeds and toss again before serving.

Myrna Swearingen   **Corona High School, Corona, CA**

Oriental Greens Salad

Serves: 4

3 cups lettuce, torn
$1/_2$ cup bok choy or spinach, shredded
$1/_2$ cup bean sprouts
$1/_4$ cup radish slices
$1/_4$ cup cashews
creamy cucumber dressing

Combine all ingredients and toss lightly. Serve with a creamy cucumber dressing.

"This salad has terrific flavor and crunch!"

Monica Blanchette   **Landmark Middle School, Moreno Valley, CA**

Quick & Easy Elegant Salad

Serves: 4

4 to 6 cups mixed salad greens
$1/_3$ cup dried cherries or cranberries
$1/_3$ cup pecans or walnuts, toasted, coarsely chopped
$1/_3$ cup Gorgonzola cheese, crumbled
$1/_3$ cup cherry tomatoes
1 red onion, thinly sliced
Newman's Raspberry Walnut Salad Dressing

Quickly combine ingredients listed or leave out what you don't like. (Sometimes I add sliced avocado or leave out tomatoes). Toss with just enough dressing to coat ingredients (you don't need much!). Arrange on chilled salad plates and serve with chilled forks.

"This is a delicious, elegant first course."

Diane Wolak   **Martin Luther King High School, Riverside, CA**

Raspberry Mango Salad

Serves: 4   *98 Cal; 8g Fat; 4g Carbs; 3g Protein*

2 cups Arugula
1 cup Bibb or Boston lettuce
$1/_2$ cup watercress, stems removed
1 cup mango, peeled, diced
$3/_4$ cup fresh raspberries
$1/_4$ cup (1.5 ounce) blue cheese, crumbled
1 tablespoon raspberry vinegar
$1/_8$ teaspoon salt
$1/_8$ teaspoon black pepper

Combine Arugula, Bibb or Boston lettuce, watercress, mango, raspberries and blue cheese in medium bowl. Shake remaining ingredients in a small jar. Pour over salad; toss to coat. Serve immediately.

"Guests love this colorful salad... nice on a hot evening.
Add chicken and you have a complete dinner!"

Wendy Duncan　　　　　　　　　　**West Covina High School, West Covina, CA**

Salad with Avocado Dressing

Serves: 4

>　1 head Bibb lettuce, torn
>　2 (medium) tomatoes, chopped
>　$1/4$ (medium) red onion, sliced
>　2 tablespoons red onion, chopped
>　1 ripe avocado, peeled, pitted
>　1 lemon, juiced
>　1 handful cilantro (about 1 tablespoon)
>　$1/2$ teaspoon coarse salt
>　2 teaspoons water
>　1 $1/2$ tablespoons virgin olive oil

Place lettuce, tomatoes and sliced onion on plate. Combine avocado with lemon juice, chopped onion, cilantro, salt and water in food processor; blend until smooth. Stream oil into dressing. Pour over lettuce.

Penny Childers　　　　　　　　　　**Ramona High School, Ramona, CA**

Spinach Salad with Raspberry Dressing

Serves: 4

>　$1/4$ cup olive oil
>　2 teaspoons Dijon or honey mustard
>　2 teaspoons raspberry flavored vinegar
>　black pepper, freshly ground, to taste
>　1 teaspoon garlic salt
>　1 teaspoon dried basil
>　2 teaspoons + $1/2$ cup sugar, divided
>　$1/8$ teaspoon salt
>　4 cups spinach
>　4 mushrooms, sliced
>　4 strawberries. sliced
>　$1/2$ (medium) red onion, sliced
>　1 cup slivered almonds

In a bowl, whisk olive oil, mustard, vinegar, pepper, garlic salt, basil, 2 teaspoons sugar and salt until combined; set aside. In another bowl, combine spinach, mushrooms, strawberries and red onion; set aside. In saute pan, add remaining $1/2$ cup sugar and heat until melted, about 6 minutes. Add almonds and stir until sugar has caramelized, stirring constantly. Remove from pan to a parchment lined sheet. Cool. Break into small pieces. Pour dressing over salad ingredients and toss; sprinkle with almonds and serve.

Penny Childers   **Ramona High School, Ramona, CA**

Springtime Salad
Serves: 8 - 10

> Cherry flavored Craisins
> green apples, cored, sliced
> Gorgonzola cheese, shredded
> 1 bag baby spinach
> 1 bag European Spring Mix salad
> apple cinnamon glazed walnuts
> celery, chopped
> Maple Grove Fat Free Poppy Seed Dressing

This is quick and easy and quite the show stopper! Slicing the apples is the only step that requires any time at all. The down side: all must be mixed at the last minute to prevent the apples from turning brown and the nuts from getting soggy.

Jan Schulenburg   **Irvine High School, Irvine, CA**

Summer Strawberry Chicken Salad
Serves: 4 - 6

> 3 tablespoons red wine vinegar
> 3 tablespoons olive oil
> 2 tablespoons Splenda
> 3 tablespoons orange juice
> $1/4$ teaspoon dry mustard
> 2 cups chicken breast, cooked, cubed
> 1 head Bibb lettuce
> 1 can Mandarin oranges, drained
> 1 cup strawberries, sliced
> 1 tablespoon cilantro, chopped

Mix vinegar, olive oil, Splenda, orange juice and dry mustard in a jar and refrigerate 2 to 3 hours. In a large salad bowl. toss together chicken breast, lettuce, oranges, strawberries and cilantro. Pour dressing over and toss again; serve.

"The Splenda in the dressing lowers the calories in this summer salad."

Angela Croce   **Mira Mesa High School, San Diego, CA**

Tabouli with a Twist

Serves: 8

    1 cup wheat bulgur
    water
    3 tomatoes, diced
    1 English cucumber, diced
    2 lemons
    2 limes
    sea salt, to taste
    pepper, to taste
    1 bunch Italian flat leaf parsley, chopped
    1 bunch curly leaf parsley, chopped
    $1/4$ bunch fresh mint leaves, chopped, stemmed

Soak the bulgur in enough hot water to cover about $3/4$" over wheat; set aside. Slice, then dice tomatoes and cucumbers to size of a pea. Slice both lemons and limes in half. Squeeze juices into large bowl with tomatoes and cucumbers. Add salt and pepper. Chop both parsleys, including stems by $1/4$". Mix with tomatoes and cucumbers. Chop mint and add. Add bulgur, if soft, to mixture (do not add too much). Taste and adjust seasonings. Serve with crackers or celery sticks.

"Best made a day ahead and chilled. Add the lime, it's very crucial to the flavor and will be boring if you don't. Excellent hot weather dish that is very refreshing. Healthy anti-oxidant rich dish that can be a side dish, salad or entreé. Tomatoes and citrus are good sources of Vitamin C; bulgur is a whole grain = fiber, energy and B vitamins!"

Victoria Star   **McClatchy High School, Sacramento, CA**

Tofu Salad

Serves: 4

    1 block tofu, cut into 1" cubes, drained
    $1/2$ head lettuce, shredded
    2 (medium) tomatoes, chopped
    1 cucumber, sliced
    3 green onions, chopped
    1 can tuna in water, drained
    1 tablespoon sesame seeds
    Dressing:
    1 tablespoon sesame oil
    $1/4$ cup canola oil
    $1/2$ cup mild soy sauce

Cut tofu into cubes; drain on paper towels. In a shallow dish, layer lettuce, tofu, tomatoes, cucumber and green onion. Top with flaked tuna and sprinkle with sesame seeds. Combine dressing ingredients in a jar. Shake well and pour over salad before serving.

"Delicious for pot lucks and family dinners. High in protein."

Reiko Ikkanda　　　　　　　　**So. Pasadena Middle School, So. Pasadena, CA**

Un-Potato Salad

Serves: 12　　　　　　　　　　　　*3g Carbs; 1g Fiber; 3g Protein*

1 (large) head cauliflower, cut into small chunks
1 tablespoon water
2 cups celery, diced
1 cup red onion, diced
2 cups mayonnaise
$1/4$ cup cider vinegar
2 teaspoons salt or Vege-Sal
2 teaspoons Splenda
$1/2$ teaspoon pepper
4 eggs, hard cooked, chopped

Put cauliflower in microwave-safe casserole with water; cover and cook on HIGH 5 to 7 minutes. Let stand 3 to 5 minutes. (Cauliflower should be tender, not mushy.) Drain cauliflower and combine with celery and onion in bowl. Combine mayonnaise, vinegar, salt, Splenda and pepper. Pour over vegetables and mix well. Stir in chopped eggs. Chill before serving.

"Great for those summer backyard parties!"

Sonja Tyree　　　　　　　　　　**Ayala High School, Chino Hills, CA**

Sauces Salsa & MARINADES

Cilantro Dipping Sauce
Makes: about 1 1/2 cups

2 bunches cilantro, trimmed, leaving some stems
2 cloves garlic, crushed
1/3 cup Macadamia nuts, toasted
1 teaspoon chili, seeded, chopped
1/2 cup extra virgin olive oil
salt and pepper, to taste

Wash and dry cilantro; place in food processor with garlic, nuts and chili. Process until finely chopped. With motor still running, add olive oil in a thin stream until well combined. Salt & pepper to taste.

"Excellent sauce for shrimp or any type of fish."

Marie Coots   **Huntington Beach High School, Huntington Beach, CA**

Easy Marinade
Serves: 8

1/2 cup soy sauce
1/4 cup canola oil
3 scallions, chopped
2 cloves garlic, crushed
pepper, to taste

Mix ingredients together. Place meat in a gallon sized ziploc bag and pour in marinade. Refrigerate to marinate 3 hours to overnight.

"Discard all uncooked marinade. I usually use this for shish kabob. Cube the meat into even sizes. Marinate, then skewer the meat before barbecuing. Soak bamboo skewers in water to prevent them from burning on barbecue."

Laurie Paolozzi   **West High School, Torrance, CA**

Honey Yogurt Dipping Sauce

Makes: 1 ¹/₂ cups

1 ¹/₂ cups plain yogurt
3 tablespoons honey
2 tablespoons fresh lemon juice
1 ¹/₂ teaspoons vanilla

Photo
opposite
page 32

In a medium bowl, whisk together all ingredients until blended.
Transfer to a serving bowl, or cover and refrigerate until ready to use.
Serve over seasonal fresh fruit.

Wisconsin Milk Marketing Board, Inc.   **Madison, WI**

Italian Sauce

Makes: 6 cups

¹/₂ cup canola oil
1 cup onion, chopped
1 clove garlic, peeled, chopped
1 (2 pound) can whole tomatoes, chopped
1 (6 ounce) can tomato sauce
1 (16 ounce) can tomato pureé
1 teaspoon parsley
1 teaspoon salt
1 teaspoon dried oregano
¹/₂ teaspoon dried basil
¹/₄ teaspoon pepper

Place oil in heavy pan on stove top. Saute onion and garlic until
golden brown. Use a paper towel to remove excess oil. Add tomatoes,
tomato sauce and pureé to sauteéd vegetables. Stir in seasonings. Cover
and simmer for at least 1 hour (or 6 hours in a crock pot). Remove lid to
allow extra liquid to evaporate and become the consistency that you
desire. Serve over hot cooked pasta or meat.

Jill Sweet-Gregory   **Santa Paula High School, Santa Paula, CA**

Mango Salsa

Serves: 11   *30 Cal; 0g Fat; 8g Carbs; 1g Fiber; 0mg Sodium*

2 ripe mangos, peeled, pitted, coarsely chopped
1 (small) red bell pepper, seeded, coarsely chopped
1 (small) red onion, minced
¹/₄ cup fresh cilantro, chopped
1 (medium) clove garlic, minced
¹/₄ cup pineapple juice
6 tablespoons fresh lime juice
1 jalapeño pepper, finely chopped

Combine all ingredients and stir well to mix. Refrigerate 1 hour before serving so flavors can blend.

"This salsa is excellent with baked fish or in fish tacos.
You can also serve it with pita or tortilla chips for an appetizer."

Holly Pittman   **El Capitan High School, Lakeside, CA**

Peach & Mango Salsa

Makes: 3 cups   *92 Cal; 1g Fat; 9g Carbs; 8g Fiber*

2 (medium) ripe, firm peaches, seeded, cut into small chunks
$1/2$ (large) mango, peeled, seeded, cut into small chunks
$1/3$ cup red pepper, finely chopped
$1/3$ cup yellow pepper, finely chopped
$1/4$ cup red onion, finely chopped
1 (small) jalapeño pepper, minced
3 tablespoons cilantro, chopped
1 tablespoon fresh lime juice
2 teaspoons olive oil
$1/4$ teaspoon salt

Mix all ingredients in a bowl and refrigerate in a covered container for at least 30 minutes and up to 3 hours before serving. Serve with roasted meats or fish, or as an accompaniment to quesadillas or tortilla chips.

"My family loves this on fish. It also goes over well with tortilla chips."

Charlene Nugent   **Petaluma Junior High School, Petaluma, CA**

Vegetables & SIDE DISHES

Beets with Orange & Ginger

Serves: 6   *115 Cal; 14g Carbs; 2g Protein; 6g Fat; 1g Fiber; 18mg Sodium*

6 (medium) beets
1 cup orange juice
2 tablespoons candied ginger
2 tablespoons maple syrup
$1/2$ cup walnuts, chopped
1 tablespoon white vinegar
1 tablespoon cornstarch

Scrub beets, leaving on root and 1" of stem. Place beets in a large pot and cover with water. Bring to a boil, cover and simmer 45 to 60 minutes or until tender; drain. Remove skins and cut beets into wedges. In a saucepan, combine remaining ingredients; bring to a boil, simmer until thickened. Add beets and toss.

"This is so good and good for you! I add fresh pineapple too. (You can use canned beets, but freshly cooked ones retain more nutrients.) Science says beets' anti-cancer chemicals inhibit skin, lung and liver tumors in mice. Beets also may help the heart by lowering artery damaging homocysteine."

Brenda Burke   **Mt. Whitney High School, Visalia, CA**

Brown Rice Primavera

Serves: 6   *176 Cal; 3g Fat; 32g Carbs; 2g Fiber; 190 mg Sodium; 6g Protein*

    nonstick cooking spray
    2 cloves garlic, minced
    2 zucchini, halved, cut into $1/_2$" thick pieces
    2 yellow crookneck squash, halved, cut into $1/_2$" pieces
    $1/_2$ teaspoon salt
    $1/_2$ teaspoon ground pepper
    $1/_4$ cup water
    3 cups brown rice, cooked (cold)
    1 (large) tomato, seeded, diced
    $1/_2$ cup fresh basil, chopped
    $1/_4$ cup Italian parsley, chopped
    $1/_4$ cup Parmesan cheese, grated

Coat a large nonstick frying pan with cooking spray and saute garlic
for 30 seconds. Add zucchini and crookneck squash, salt and pepper;
saute 3 minutes. Stir in water, cover and cook until vegetables are tender,
about 3 minutes. Uncover and add rice. Cook 3 to 4 minutes. Stir in
tomato, basil, parsley and cheese. Salt to taste.

"A great accompaniment to fish or chicken."

Millie Deeton   **Ayala High School, Chino Hills, CA**

Creamy Cauliflower-Pea Medley

Serves: 4   *104 Cal; 2.4g Fat; 15.7g Carbs; 5.1g Fiber; 6g Protein; 213mg Sodium; 3mg Chol.*

    $1/_2$ cup water
    1 (10 ounce) package frozen cauliflower
    1 (10 ounce) package frozen peas
    1 cup cucumber, peeled, diced
    3 tablespoons reduced fat California Ranch Dressing
    2 teaspoons nonfat sour cream substitute
    $1/_4$ teaspoon dried whole dillweed

Combine first 3 ingredients in saucepan; bring to a boil. Cover and
cook 5 minutes; drain well. Combine cauliflower mixture and remaining
ingredients in a bowl; toss well. Serve warm or chilled.

Debi Spencer   **Colton High School, Colton, CA**

Eggplant Italian Style

Serves: 6

> 2 (medium) eggplant
> $1/3$ cup olive oil
> 2 cups celery, chopped
> 2 cups onion, chopped
> $1/2$ teaspoon garlic salt
> $1/2$ teaspoon seasoned salt
> 2 (14.5 ounce) cans Italian stewed tomatoes

Cut eggplant into 1" cubes and soak in salted water for 30 minutes; drain and pat dry. Saute eggplant in olive oil until translucent; remove to paper towels to drain and set aside. Saute celery and onion in olive oil and seasonings; add Italian stewed tomatoes and drained eggplant. Simmer 20 to 30 minutes. Serve over hot pasta (if not counting Carbs) or serve alone.

"This is so good and healthy for you! Our wonderful neighbor, Ginny Stone, served it to us at their Super Bowl Potluck!"

Brenda Burke   **Mt. Whitney High School, Visalia, CA**

Fabulous French Fries

Serves: 3

> 3 (large) potatoes
> 1 egg white
> nonstick cooking spray

Scrub or peel potatoes and cut into thick, French-fry strips. Beat egg whites until foamy. Add potato strips and coat well. Spread potatoes in a single layer on a cookie sheet that has been sprayed with nonstick cooking spray. Bake 30 to 35 minutes or until potatoes are crispy. Sprinkle with salt. Note: Sprinkle with Parmesan cheese, garlic powder or salt, lemon pepper or Salad Supreme before baking. Use russets or sweet potatoes.

"My family loves homemade french-fries. These are a good substitute without all the oil."

Camille Hicks   **Riverton High School, Riverton, UT**

Fantastic Fruit with Yogurt Dressing

Makes: 6 cups

> 6 cups fresh fruit, diced (Choose fruits of varying color such as
>   strawberries, cantaloupe, apples, grapes, kiwi,
>   Mandarin oranges, raisins)
> 2 (8 ounce) containers lowfat vanilla yogurt
> $1/4$ teaspoon almond extract
> 2 to 4 tablespoons honey

Clean and dice your fruit selection. Some canned fruit is good to use in this, especially during the winter when fresh selections are limited. For example, canned pineapple and Mandarin oranges are great for taste and additional color variety. Combine yogurt and extract completely. Add only 2 tablespoons of honey first, then taste. Yogurt sweetness varies by brand. Add more, if necessary. Also, consider how sweet and/or flavorful your fruit is. To serve, place a serving of fruit into a bowl and top with a dollop of dressing. Don't dress the entire salad with dressing as it tends to become watery when left sitting.

"High in fiber, vitamins and minerals, essential for life long health and fitness. A great way to incorporate your daily fruit servings into a meal. My family loves it!"

Delaine Smith   **West Valley High School, Cottonwood, CA**

Greek Omelet

Serves: 2

    nonstick cooking spray
    2 whole eggs
    4 egg whites
    $1/4$ teaspoon salt
    fresh basil, snipped
    2 tablespoons lowfat feta cheese, crumbled
    1 Roma tomato, chopped

Spray an omelet skillet with nonstick cooking spray. In a bowl, whisk eggs, egg whites and salt. Pour into skillet and cook over low-medium heat. Using a spatula, lift edges and slide uncooked portion underneath. Add tomato, cheese and basil. Gently slide omelet onto plate, folding top in half.

"To reduce cholesterol and fat, use an egg substitute."

Kristi Melton   **Marina High School, Huntington Beach, CA**

Green Beans & Feta with Dill

Serves: 5

    1 pound fresh green beans
    $1/4$ cup fat free Italian salad dressing
    $1/4$ cup feta cheese, crumbled
    2 tablespoons red onion, chopped
    2 tablespoons fresh dill, chopped

Cook beans in boiling water 7 minutes or until tender-crisp; drain and rinse with cold water. Toss with dressing, cheese, onion and dill in large bowl. Serve immediately or refrigerate several hours until chilled.

"Lowfat and a good source of Vitamins A and C and fiber. Also low in sodium."

Jill Burnham   **Bloomington High School, Bloomington, CA**

Guacamole

Makes: 3 cups

1 (16 ounce) container lowfat or fat free cottage cheese
3 ripe avocados, peeled pitted
$1/2$ jar salsa
salt and pepper, to taste
$1/4$ cup onion, chopped (optional)

Drain any liquid off cottage cheese. Blend all ingredients together in a bowl, and you're ready to serve!

"Great dip for chips and veggies. High in nutrients and low in fat!"

Kathie Hogen   **Hendrix Junior High School, Mesa, AZ**

Italian Vegetables

Serves: 6   *50 Cal; 5 Carbs*

4 cups broccoli florets
$1/2$ cup water
$1/2$ teaspoon Italian seasoning
$1/2$ teaspoon dried parsley
$1/4$ teaspoon salt
$1/8$ teaspoon pepper
2 Roma tomatoes, cut into wedges
$1/2$ cup Mozzarella cheese, shredded

Place broccoli and water in a 2 quart microwave casserole dish; cover. Microwave on HIGH 5 to 8 minutes; drain. Toss with seasonings and tomato wedges. Microwave, uncovered, 2 to 4 minutes on HIGH. Sprinkle with cheese. Microwave 1 minute more to melt cheese.

"Tasty and colorful"

Cathy Miller   **Montclair High School, Montclair, CA**

Lemon Herb Broccoli

Serves: 2 to 3   *118 Cal; 8g Fat; 192mg Sodium; 0mg Cholesterol*

1 bunch broccoli, cut into florets
2 tablespoons margarine
3 to 4 tablespoons lemon juice
1 tablespoon Dijon mustard
$1/2$ teaspoon dried marjoram, crumbled

Steam broccoli until tender-crisp. Melt margarine in saucepan over medium heat. Blend in lemon juice, mustard and marjoram. Spoon over broccoli.

"Serve with grilled chicken breasts or broiled fish steaks."

Kathie Baczynski   **Mt. Carmel High School, Poway, CA**

Lowfat Potato Casserole

Serves: 9   **Weight Watchers 1 cup = 1 point**

$1/2$ cup green onion, chopped
1 cup reduced-fat cheddar cheese, shredded
2 tablespoons margarine, melted
$1/2$ teaspoon pepper
1 (32 ounce) bag frozen hash browns
1 (16 ounce) carton fat free sour cream
1 (10 ounce) can reduced fat cream of chicken soup
$1/2$ teaspoon onion salt
nonstick cooking spray
$1/2$ teaspoon paprika

Preheat oven to 350 degrees. Combine first 8 ingredients in large bowl; stir well to mix. Spray a 9" x 13" pan with nonstick cooking spray. Spoon mixture into pan. Sprinkle paprika evenly over all; bake 1 hour.

"A good lowfat version of Funeral Potatoes!"

Paulette Evans   **Cyprus High School, Magna, UT**

Mashed Cauliflower

Serves: 4

1 head cauliflower, washed, chopped
1 clove garlic
3 ounces cream cheese
1 to 2 tablespoons butter
3 ounces sour cream
salt and pepper, to taste

Boil or steam cauliflower and garlic until quite tender. (Be sure cauliflower is VERY tender!). Drain; mash with cream cheese, butter and enough sour cream to desired consistency. Add salt and pepper to taste. Note: This recipe makes a great Shepherd's Pie topping. It is very low in carbohydrates and makes a good substitute for mashed potatoes.

Debby Truitt   **Woodland High School, Woodland, CA**

No Fry French Fries

Serves: 4

nonstick cooking spray
2 pounds (large) baking potatoes
1 tablespoon vegetable oil
1 clove garlic, minced
1 teaspoon salt
$1/4$ teaspoon ground black pepper

Beef Stuffed Peppers **Page 74**

Sesame-Soy Beef Stir Fry **Page 78**

Preheat oven to 450 degrees. Line a baking sheet with aluminum foil. Coat foil generously with nonstick cooking spray. Scrub potatoes; pat dry. Cut each lengthwise into $1/2$" thick slices, then into $1/2$" wide strips. Toss potatoes on baking sheet with garlic, salt and pepper until well coated. Bake 40 to 45 minutes, turning once or twice with spatula, until potatoes are crisp and golden.

Gini Knowles   **Murrieta Valley High School, Murrieta, CA**

Quick and Easy Marinated Green Beans

Serves: 4   *30 Cal.*

1 (14.5 ounce) can cut green beans, no salt added, drained
$1/4$ cup red onion, sliced
$1/2$ cup extra lite Italian dressing
$1/4$ cup red kidney beans, drained (optional)
$1/4$ cup garbanzo beans, drained (optional)

Toss beans with sliced onion and dressing. Cover and refrigerate approximately 1 hour before serving. Toss just before serving.
NOTE; You may substitute red wine vinegar and canola or olive oil plus chopped garlic for the Italian dressing.

"This is very quick and easy to prepare. It makes a cool accompaniment to lasagna or any barbecue fare."

Janet Policy   **Ramona High School, Riverside, CA**

Refrigerator Pickles

Makes: 2 quarts

7 cups cucumbers, peeled, seeded, sliced
1 cup sweet onion, sliced
1 teaspoon celery seed
2 cups sugar
2 teaspoons salt
1 cup white or cider vinegar

Combine cucumbers and onion in a large non-metal bowl. Add celery seed, sugar, salt and vinegar; mix well. Cover and refrigerate at least 24 hours before serving. You can vary the taste by adding bell pepper, garlic, dill, fresh herbs or hot peppers.
Note: This will keep in the refrigerates for 2 to 4 weeks.

"This is a nice lowfat snack and a good way to use all those cucumbers if you grown your own.'"

Shauna Young   **Jordan High School, Sandy, UT**

Roasted Vegetable Medley

Serves: 8   *130 Cal; 7g Fat; 17g Carbs; 3g Protein; 65mg Sodium*

    2 zucchini
    1 red bell pepper
    1 green bell pepper
    2 summer squash (Patty Pan)
    2 yellow crookneck squash
    1 (6") square banana squash, peeled
    1 Japanese eggplant
    1 (medium) purple onion
    1/4 cup olive oil
    1/2 teaspoon garlic salt
    1/4 teaspoon black pepper

Preheat oven to 325 degrees. Wash all vegetables and cut into 1"
pieces. Place in a 9" x 13" glass baking dish. Drizzle with olive oil and
sprinkle with garlic salt and pepper. Toss gently. Bake, uncovered,
approximately 1 hour.

*"Easy to make and gives loads of vitamins and phytochemicals. By not using
potatoes, pumpkin or corn, this fits right into the South Beach way of eating!"*
Laurie Paolozzi   **West High School, Torrance, CA**

Sautéed Apples & Squash

Serves: 6 - 8

    2 teaspoons olive oil
    4 cups banana squash, peeled, diced (or any winter squash)
    2 Granny Smith apples, peeled, diced
    1 (small) sweet onion, diced
    1/2 teaspoon cinnamon
    1/2 teaspoon cardamom
    1/2 teaspoon coriander
    1 teaspoon sugar
    salt and pepper, to taste

In a nonstick saute pan, heat olive oil. Add squash and saute until
evenly browned on all sides. Add apples and onion and continue to
saute. As the squash and apples become tender, add spices. Continue
cooking until squash and apples are tender. Serve immediately.

*"This is a wonderful change for a vegetable side dish. It has a Middle Eastern
flavor from the spices and goes well with many other dishes.
Created in desperation for a potluck dinner and was the hit of the evening!"*
Pam Bonilla   **Valley View High School, Moreno Valley, CA**

Spanish Rice

Serves: 8

2 1/2 cups dry brown rice
5 cups water
1 pound hamburger
1 cup salsa
1 (8 ounce) can tomato sauce
Toppings: Tabasco sauce, cheese chunks, black olives, green onions,
    sour cream, guacamole

Cook rice by combining with water and simmering over medium heat, covered, until water is absorbed and rice is tender, approximately 20 minutes. Brown hamburger in fry pan; drain. Stir in cooked rice, salsa and tomato sauce; mix well. Heat over medium heat, stirring frequently. Serve as a main dish or side dish with optional toppings.

"The brown rice adds high nutrition and a unique texture."

Cheryl Moyle   **Olympus High School, Salt Lake City, UT**

Stuffed Tomatoes

Serves: 6 - 8   *125 Cal; 5g Fat; 65mg Sodium; 2mg Cholesterol*

6 to 8 (medium) firm tomatoes
2 tablespoons oil
1/3 cup celery, chopped
2 tablespoons onion, chopped
2 cups brown rice, cooked
1/4 cup Parmesan cheese, grated
1 tablespoon fresh parsley, snipped
1 teaspoon dried basil
1/8 teaspoon black pepper
1/8 teaspoon garlic powder

Cut thin slices from top of each tomato; set aside. Scrape out center of tomatoes; chop pulp and set aside. Place shells, upside down, on paper towels to drain. Preheat oven to 350 degrees. Heat oil in medium saucepan. Add celery and onion; saute over moderate heat until celery is tender. Remove from heat. Add reserved tomato pulp, rice, Parmesan cheese, parsley, basil, pepper and garlic powder; mix well. Fill each tomato shell with rice mixture. Replace tops, if desired. Lightly oil a 9"pie plate or round baking dish. Place tomatoes in dish; cover with aluminum foil. Bake 30 to 45 minutes or until tomatoes are tender.

*"Use 1 lightly oiled custard cup for each tomato instead
of a pie plate or baking dish, if desired."*

Kathie Baczynski   **Mt. Carmel High School, Poway, CA**

Sugar Snap Peas
Serves: 4

> 3/4 to 1 pound sugar snap peas
> 1 1/2 teaspoons oil
> 1 1/2 teaspoons rice vinegar
> 1/4 teaspoon fresh ginger, grated
> salt and pepper, to taste

Cook sugar snap peas in boiling water until tender-crisp, about 2 to 3 minutes. Rinse under cold water and drain to stop cooking process. Toss peas with oil, vinegar, ginger, salt and pepper.

"I enjoy sugar snap peas and always add more to each serving to help satisfy hungry appetites. I enjoy them plain and it's hard not to eat too many before they are cooked!"

Barbara Allen　　　　　　　　　　　　　　**Ayala High School, Chino Hills, CA**

Tangy Lime Risotto
Serves: 8　　　　　　　　　　　　　　　　　　　　　　　　　**3g Fat**

> 1 cup Arborio rice, uncooked or short-grain white rice, rinsed, drained
> 1/4 cup onion, chopped
> 2 teaspoons olive oil
> 3 1/2 cups hot water
> 2 tablespoons fresh lime juice
> 1 1/2 teaspoons instant chicken bouillon granules
> 1 cup frozen baby peas and mushrooms
>   or other vegetables of your choice
> 1/4 cup Parmesan cheese, freshly grated
> 1 tablespoon parsley, snipped

Combine rice, onion and oil in 12" nonstick skillet. Cook over medium heat for 6 to 8 minutes or just until rice begins to brown, stirring constantly. Add hot water, juice and bouillon. Simmer 20 to 25 minutes or until rice is tender and water is nearly absorbed, stirring occasionally. Stir in peas and mushrooms, cheese and parsley. Cook 3 to 4 minutes or until peas are hot and texture is creamy, stirring frequently.

"Arborio rice is traditionally used for risotto because of the high starch content which gives the dish its creamy texture. I joined the Women's Health Initiative over 4 years ago and have learned a lot."

Carole Call　　　　　　　　　　　**Costa Mesa High School, Costa Mesa, CA**

Tomatoes in Basil & Balsamic Vinegar

Serves: 1 - 2

2 tomatoes, sliced
4 fresh basil leaves, chopped
$1/4$ cup balsamic vinegar
salt and pepper, to taste

Arrange sliced tomatoes and basil leaves on serving plate. Splash with vinegar and season with salt and pepper. Allow to sit, unrefrigerated 2 to 3 hours before serving.

"During the months when tomatoes are not in season, I use a high quality whole canned tomato."

Terry Kluever   **Coronado High School, Henderson, NV**

Twice Baked Squash

Serves: 4

2 acorn or butternut squash
$1/2$ cup Parmesan cheese, grated, divided
1 cup lowfat cottage cheese
4 egg whites
$1/2$ cup instant mashed potato flakes
$1/2$ cup green onions, minced
1 teaspoon fresh lemon juice
$1/2$ cup seasoned croutons

Preheat oven to 350 degrees. Cut squash in half and remove seeds. Place in a shallow baking dish, cover with foil and bake 45 to 60 minutes. Scoop pulp from squash leaving a shell approximately $1/3$" thick. Place the scooped out pulp, all but 2 tablespoons Parmesan cheese, cottage cheese, egg whites, potato flakes, green onions and lemon juice into a mixer bowl. Mix on low until well blended. Spoon mixture into squash shells. Sprinkle with reserved Parmesan cheese and croutons. Place in shallow baking pan. Return to oven and bake 35 to 40 minutes or until knife inserted in center comes out clean.

"If you don't think you like squash, try this recipe and you will be pleasantly surprised! I thank Sue Stanley for this recipe."

Leah Brown   **Marina High School, Huntington Beach, CA**

Unfried Cheese Fries

Serves: 6   *147 Cal; 1.7g Fat; 28.9g Carbs; 2.1g Fiber; 4.4g Protein; 190mg Sodium; 4mg. Chol.*

1 $^1/_2$ pounds baking potatoes, unpeeled,
    cut into thin strips (about 3 potatoes)
nonstick cooking spray
$^1/_4$ cup Parmesan cheese, grated
$^1/_4$ teaspoon salt
$^1/_4$ teaspoon pepper
$^1/_4$ teaspoon paprika

Preheat oven to 450 degrees. Coat potato strips with cooking spray and place in a large, heavy-duty ziploc plastic bag. Combine cheese and remaining 3 ingredients; sprinkle over potato strips in bag. Seal bag and turn to coat potatoes well. Arrange potato strips in a single layer on a large baking sheet that has been coated with nonstick cooking spray. Bake 15 minutes, turning once. Serve immediately.

"Delicious fries that aren't fried, but baked.
You can munch away guiltlessly. Serve with reduced calorie catsup."

Jan Tuttle   **Mills High School, Millbrae, CA**

Vegetable Casserole

Serves: 6 - 8

2 cups broccoli pieces
1 cup carrots, sliced
1 cup zucchini, sliced
1 cup eggplant, cubed
1 cup green beans
2 cups cooked rice or noodles (optional)
1 $^1/_2$ cups spaghetti sauce
1 cup longhorn cheese, shredded
1 cup Monterey jack cheese, shredded

Combine vegetables and steam 5 to 7 minutes. Layer bottom of casserole dish with rice or pasta (if using). Layer vegetables on top of rice. Spread spaghetti sauce on top. Bake at 375 degrees for 30 minutes. Combine cheeses and sprinkle on top. Return to oven just long enough to melt cheese.

"I love this dish because I can change it to suit what I have on hand.
Can even add cooked chicken to layer the bottom with cooked rice."

Pat Johnson   **Iron Horse Middle School, San Ramon, CA**

Vegetable Frittata

6 eggs
2 tablespoons milk
1 tablespoon butter or oil
Use the following in desired amounts:
bell peppers, chopped
onion, chopped
potato, chopped
green onions, chopped
tomato, chopped
mushrooms, sliced
bacon (cooked)
Monterey jack or cheddar cheese, shredded

Preheat oven to 350 degrees. Combine eggs and milk; whisk to combine. Heat butter or oil in ovenproof skillet. Add desired vegetables and cook 1 to 2 minutes or until tender. Add egg mixture, cheese and cooked bacon. Cook over low heat until bottom starts to set. Lift edges with a pancake turner and tilt skillet to allow uncooked egg to run to the bottom. Place skillet in oven for 5 to 10 minutes or until no longer moist and eggs are cooked. Slice frittata onto plate or cutting board. Slice into wedges and serve.

"Great for a Sunday brunch or even dinner!"

Mary Keane-Gruener   **Hoover High School, Glendale, CA**

Vegetable Garden Medley

Serves: 4

1 to 2 cups broccoli florets
1 to 2 cups cauliflower florets
3 carrots, cut into 2' chunks, sliced lengthwise
6 (medium) mushrooms
4 to 6 tablespoons butter or margarine
$1/_8$ teaspoon garlic salt
dash white pepper

Arrange broccoli and cauliflower around outer edge of a glass pie plate. Lay carrot slices on top. Place mushrooms in center of dish. Cover with plastic wrap and microwave on HIGH 4 to 5 minutes, rotating dish once. Let stand 2 minutes. While vegetables are standing, place butter, garlic salt and pepper in a glass dish. Microwave on HIGH 30 to 45 seconds or until butter melts; stir to blend. Pour over vegetables and serve.

"We use this in our microwave unit. The students always turn their noses up at first, but end up eating every little bit! It is quick, easy, delicious and healthy!"

Laura Lewis   **Garden Grove High School, Garden Grove, CA**

Zucchini and Tomato Gratin

Serves: 6

3 (medium) zucchini
1 tablespoon olive oil
1 tablespoon fresh parsley, chopped
1 clove garlic, minced
$1/2$ teaspoon fresh thyme
$1/4$ teaspoon fresh rosemary, minced
$1/4$ teaspoon salt
$1/8$ teaspoon pepper
4 to 6 plum tomatoes, thinly sliced
2 tablespoons bread crumbs

Heat oven to 400 degrees. Cut zucchini into $1/4$" slices. In large bowl, toss zucchini with olive oil, parsley, garlic, thyme, rosemary, salt and pepper. In a Gratin dish, alternate layers of zucchini with tomatoes. Cover with foil and bake 30 minutes. Remove foil. Sprinkle with bread crumbs and bake 20 minutes more.

Leah Brown   **Marina High School, Huntington Beach, CA**

Main Dishes With BEEF

Beef Stroganoff

Serves: 4

1 pound London broil
2 to 3 tablespoons canola margarine or olive oil
$^1/_2$ pound mushrooms, fresh, sliced
1 (medium) onion, thinly sliced
2 bouillon cubes, dissolved in 2 cups water
$^1/_2$ teaspoon fresh garlic, minced
3 tablespoons flour
1 cup fat free sour cream
3 to 4 cups noodles, cooked, hot
1 to 2 tablespoons parsley, fresh

Cut meat across grain into $^1/_4$" x 1 $^1/_2$" strips. Melt margarine or oil in large skillet. Add mushrooms and onion; cook until tender, stirring constantly; remove from skillet. In same skillet, cook meat until lightly browned. Reserving $^1/_3$ cup broth, stir in remaining broth and garlic; cover and simmer 15 minutes. Blend reserved broth and flour; stir into meat mixture. Add mushrooms and onions. Heat to a boil, stirring constantly. Boil and stir 1 minute. Reduce heat. Stir in sour cream. Serve over hot, cooked noodles, garnished with parsley.

Note: Cook noodles in boiling water (uncovered) for 4 to 6 minutes or until tender. Be sure water is boiling before adding noodles to prevent sticking and over cooking.

"If you do not have noodles, serve over hot, cooked rice. Serve with a fresh spinach salad, garnished with sliced almonds and a fresh fruit cup for dessert. A balanced, nutritious meal."

Judith Topp   **A.B. Miller High School, Fontana, CA**

Beef Stuffed Peppers

Serves: 4

> 4 (medium) green, red or yellow bell peppers
> 1 pound ground beef
> $3/4$ cup onion, chopped
> $1/4$ cup regular white rice, uncooked
> 4 tablespoons catsup, divided
> $1/2$ teaspoon salt
> 1 teaspoon dried oregano, divided
> $1/4$ teaspoon pepper
> 1 (14.5 ounce) can Italian-style stewed tomatoes, undrained

Photo opposite page 64

Preheat oven to 350 degrees. Cut tops off bell peppers; remove seeds. Combine ground beef, onion, rice, 3 tablespoons catsup, salt, $1/2$ teaspoon oregano and pepper in large bowl, mixing lightly but thoroughly. Spoon into peppers; stand peppers in an 8" x 8" baking dish. Combine remaining catsup and oregano with stewed tomatoes; pour over peppers. Cover dish tightly with aluminum foil. Bake 1 $1/2$ hours to medium doneness, until beef is no longer pink and juices run clear.

National Cattlemen's Beef Assoc.   **Chicago, IL**

Easy Beef Steak Diane

Serves: 4

> 1 tablespoon vegetable oil
> $1/2$ pound (small) mushrooms, sliced
> 2 tablespoons shallots or green onion, finely chopped
> 2 boneless beef top loin steaks,
>   cut into 1" thick pieces (about 1 $1/4$ pounds)
> 1 teaspoon lemon peel, grated
> $1/4$ teaspoon pepper
> 1 tablespoon brandy (optional)
> $1/4$ cup half & half
> 1 tablespoon from lemon juice
> 2 teaspoons Dijon mustard
> 2 teaspoons Worcestershire sauce

Heat oil in large nonstick skillet over medium heat until hot. Add mushrooms and shallots; cook and stir 3 minutes or until tender; remove. Wipe skillet with paper towels; spray with cooking spray. Heat over medium heat until hot. Combine lemon peel and pepper; press onto beef steaks. Place steaks in skillet; cook 12 to 15 minutes for medium rare to medium doneness, turning occasionally. Remove; keep warm. Add brandy to skillet; cook and stir until browned bits attached to skillet are dissolved. Stir in half & half, lemon juice, mustard and

Worcestershire sauce. Stir in mushroom mixture; heat through. Carve
steaks; serve with sauce.

National Cattlemen's Beef Assoc.   **Chicago, IL**

Fajitas

Serves: 4 - 6

$1/2$ pound round steak, thinly sliced
garlic salt
fresh cracked pepper
paprika
chili powder
cumin
whole oregano
salt
few drops Lea & Perrins Worcestershire Sauce
1 tablespoon oil
1 onion, sliced, julienned
4 slices jalapeño pepper, minced
$1/2$ red bell pepper, cut into strips
$1/2$ green pepper, cut into strips
1 to 2 green onions, thinly chopped
4 to 6 flour tortillas
Garnish: Avocado slices; cilantro sprigs

Slice meat across grain into thin slices. Coat with spices and
Worcestershire sauce to marinate. Heat oil in skillet or wok until hot.
Quickly cook meat until done; remove from pan and add sliced onion
and jalapeño pepper. Cook until onions are caramelized. Add bell
peppers and cook until slightly softened, but still retains color. Add
green onion. Add meat back to pan to rewarm. Heat flour tortillas over
gas fire on both sides. Fill with fajita mixture, add garnishes if desired
and roll.

"Works equally well with chicken breast, pork tenderloin or shrimp."

Debbie Greenwood   **Glendale High School, Glendale, CA**

Lite Taco Salad

Serves: 4   *300 Cal; 9g Fat*

$1/3$ cup onion, diced
1 clove garlic, minced
$1/2$ pound lean ground beef
4 ounces tomato sauce
1 tablespoon water
$1/2$ teaspoon salt
$1/2$ teaspoon chili powder
2 cups lettuce, shredded
1 cup baked corn chips
1 green onion, sliced
1 tomato, diced
$1/2$ cup olives, sliced
$1/2$ cup kidney beans
$1/2$ cup lowfat cheese, grated
salsa

In a skillet, cook onion and garlic with ground beef until browned; drain well. Add next 4 ingredients and cook over low heat for 10 minutes; cool. Place lettuce in salad bowl, add meat mixture and remaining ingredients in layered fashion. Serve with salsa.

"We do this in our lowfat/low calorie unit and the students really love it!"
Joanne Montoy   **Esperanza High School, Anaheim, CA**

Low Calorie Quickie Calzone

Serves: 5

$1/2$ pound lean ground beef
salt, pepper and garlic, to taste
1 cup vegetables, (onions, bell peppers, mushrooms, olives, tomatoes)
1 tablespoon butter
2 cups spaghetti sauce
1 can biscuit dough
2 tablespoons flour
$1/4$ to $1/2$ cup lowfat Mozzarella cheese, shredded

Preheat oven to 350 degrees. Cook ground beef with salt, pepper and garlic in saucepan until well done. Drain fat. Cut up desired vegetables and saute together in butter until tender crisp. Combine vegetables with cooked meat. Warm spaghetti sauce. Add a small portion of vegetable and meat mixture to sauce, about 2 tablespoons. This gives the sauce some added flavor. Roll out biscuit dough into an oval or circular shape, about 3" to 4" in diameter, on a lightly floured surface. One biscuit for the top and one for the bottom of each calzone. Place bottom dough on a lightly greased cookie sheet; fill with vegetable/meat mixture, 1 tablespoon sauce mix and cheese. Save some cheese to top the calzone.

Cover with top dough and seal edges. Bake at 350 degrees for 15 to 20 minutes. Calzone should be golden brown. Top with sauce, then sprinkle with cheese.

Deanna Saporetti   **Lemoore High School, Lemoore, CA**

Mexican Beef Stew

Serves:

2 tablespoons vegetable oil
2 $^1/_2$ pounds beef stew meat, cut into 1" pieces
2 (large) onions, chopped
4 cloves garlic, crushed
2 cans beef broth
1 cup mild or medium picante sauce
2 (medium) zucchini, thinly sliced
4 teaspoons cornstarch, dissolved in $^1/_4$ cup water
2 (small) Roma tomatoes
1 can olive, sliced, drained

In Dutch oven, heat oil over medium heat until hot. Add beef, onion and garlic; brown, stirring occasionally. Pour off drippings. Stir broth and picante sauce into beef. Bring to a boil, reduce heat to low. Cover tightly and simmer 1 $^1/_2$ hours. Add zucchini to stew. Cover and continue cooking 10 minutes. Stir in cornstarch mixture; bring to a boil over medium heat and cook 2 minutes. Stir in tomatoes and olives. Remove from heat and let stand 5 minutes. Serve with crusty French bread and salad.

Kris Hawkins   **Clovis West High School, Fresno, CA**

Roast Beef with Bleu Cheese Salad

Serves: 4   *170 Cal; 7g Fat; 13g Carbs; 3g Fiber*

$^1/_2$ pound deli roast beef, thinly sliced
8 cups spring salad greens
1 basket cherry tomatoes (about 2 dozen)
1 ounce bleu cheese, crumbled
$^1/_3$ cup fat free raspberry vinaigrette dressing

Roll slices of roast beef and slice into 1" sections. Divide greens among 4 plates and arrange $^1/_4$ of beef atop each. Add tomatoes and bleu cheese. Drizzle vinaigrette over salad.

"Great main dish salad to serve friends for a summer lunch!
Add some fresh raspberries for an even healthier meal!"

Patty Bulat   **Rogers Middle School, Long Beach, CA**

Sesame Soy Beef Stir Fry

Serves: 4

Photo opposite page 65

3 tablespoons soy sauce
2 teaspoons dark sesame oil
1 pound beef round tip steaks, cut $1/8$" to $1/4$" thick
1 (16 ounce) package frozen stir-fry vegetable mixture
$1/4$ cup water
2 teaspoons cornstarch, dissolved in $1/3$ cup water
2 cups hot cooked rice (optional)
$1/4$ cup walnuts, chopped, toasted (optional)

Combine soy sauce and sesame oil in medium bowl. Remove and reserve 2 tablespoons; set aside. Stack beef steaks, cut lengthwise in half, then crosswise into 1" wide strips. Add beef to remaining marinade; toss. Heat large nonstick skillet over medium-high heat until hot. Add half of beef; stir fry 1 minute or until outside of surface is no longer pink (do not overcook). Remove and repeat with remaining beef. Combine vegetables and water in same skillet; cook over medium-high heat 4 to 5 minutes or until most of water is evaporated and vegetables are hot, stirring occasionally. Combine cornstarch with water, stirring until smooth; add to reserved 2 tablespoons marinade. Stir into vegetables and cook, stirring 1 minute or until thickened and bubbly. Add beef; heat through. Serve over hot, cooked rice, if desired. Sprinkle with walnuts.

National Cattlemen's Beef Assoc.   **Chicago, IL**

Shredded Beef Sandwiches

Serves: 9   324 Cal; 9.4g fat; 24.5g Carbs; 1.2g Fiber; 32.2g Protein; 435mg Sodium; 87mg Chol.

1 (3.25 pound) lean, boneless chuck roast
$1/3$ cup white vinegar
$1/2$ teaspoon salt
$1/4$ teaspoon ground cloves
$1/8$ teaspoon garlic powder
3 bay leaves
9 (1.5 ounce) hamburger buns, split
9 leaves lettuce

Trim fat from roast. Place roast and next 6 ingredients in a slow cooker. Cover and cook over low heat for 11 hours or until roast is tender. Remove roast and let stand 10 minutes. Separate into bite-sized pieces and shred with forks; set aside. Strain cooking liquid; discard solids. Cover and freeze at least 1 hour. Skim fat from surface of cooking liquid; discard. Place cooking liquid in a saucepan and bring to a boil; remove from heat. Line bottom half of each bun with a lettuce leaf. Top each with shredded beef and half of bun. Serve hot cooking liquid as a dipping sauce.

"Produces it own "au Jus". A delicious, hot dip for the sandwich. Perfect for a busy day!"

Debi Spencer   **Colton High School, Colton, CA**

Stuffed Peppers

Serves: 6   *approximately 1g Carbs per serving*

3 green peppers, cut in half
1 teaspoon salt
$1/_8$ teaspoon pepper
1 tablespoon Worcestershire sauce
$1/_3$ cup oats, uncooked
1 egg, beaten
1 (8 ounce) can tomato sauce
$1/_4$ onion, finely chopped
1 $1/_2$ pounds ground beef
catsup (optional)

Cook green pepper halves in boiling salted water for 5 minutes. Invert and drain thoroughly. Combine salt, pepper, Worcestershire, oats, egg, tomato sauce and onion. Add ground beef and mix thoroughly. Pack into pepper halves. Place in a 12" by 8" baking dish. Top with a dollop of catsup, if desired. Bake at 350 degrees for 35 minutes.

"I learned to love nutritious green peppers using this recipe! A great summer time dish!"

Monica Blanchette   **Landmark Middle School, Moreno Valley, CA**

Stuffed Shells

Serves: 4

20 jumbo shells
4 ounces lean ground beef
$1/_4$ cup onion, finely chopped
$1/_2$ cup green pepper, chopped
2 cloves garlic, minced
2 ounces part-skim ricotta cheese
$1/_2$ teaspoon dried oregano
1 $1/_2$ tablespoons fresh basil, chopped
1 (14 ounce) jar spaghetti sauce, divided
2 tablespoons Parmesan cheese, grated

Preheat oven to 350 degrees. Cook shells in a large pot of boiling water just until tender. Drain and set aside. Crumble beef into a nonstick pan. Cook over medium-high heat, breaking up meat with a wooden spoon for 4 to 5 minutes or until lightly browned. Line a platter with several thicknesses of paper towels. Transfer beef to plate and drain well. Wipe out the pan with paper towel. Return beef to pan and add onions, peppers and garlic and cook 5 to 6 minutes or until onions are soft. Remove from heat. Stir in ricotta, oregano, basil and about 10 ounces of sauce. Spread a thin layer of sauce on bottom of a 9" x 13" pan. Stuff mixture into cooked shells and place shells in pan; top with remaining sauce and Parmesan. Bake 30 minutes or until heated through.

"Try ground turkey instead of beef."

Amy Dedini   **Linden High School, Linden, CA**

Veal Cutlets a la Vegetables

Serves: 4

> 8 ounces veal, sliced
> Spike All-Purpose Seasoning - No Salt
> 1 (medium) onion, thinly sliced
> 15 fresh beans, straight cut
> 1 fresh carrot, roll cut
> 10 stalks asparagus, cut diagonally
> 1 (small) crookneck squash, sliced julienne
> $1/_2$ cup baby corn, cut
> 4 to 5 artichoke hearts, cut into fourths
> 2 tablespoons olive oil
> 1 (12 ounce) jar mushroom gravy
> 1 cup mozzarella cheese, grated

Preheat oven to 350 degrees. Season veal slices with Spike seasoning; set aside. Prepare all vegetables; set aside. Cut and saute onion in olive oil until tender and golden. Push to sides of skillet and add veal slices. Brown each side lightly. Remove veal and onion and place in a lightly greased oblong baking dish. Cover with foil and bake 10 minutes. Add mushroom gravy and continue baking 10 minutes or until heated through. Add vegetables and replace cover; continue baking another 10 minutes, or until vegetables are tender-crisp (do not overcook). Remove foil and sprinkle with finely grated mozzarella cheese. Bake until cheese melts. Remove from oven and serve hot.

"The more color and variety of fresh crisp cooked vegetables, the more vitamins and minerals you get. Over cooking destroys color, flavor and nutrients."

Judith Topp   **A. B. Miller High School, Fontana, CA**

Zucchini Lasagna

Serves: 6 - 8

8 ounces cream cheese
1 cup cottage cheese
1 cup sour cream
$1/4$ cup onion, chopped
$1/4$ cup green pepper, chopped
1 $1/2$ pounds ground beef
$1/2$ teaspoon oregano
$1/2$ teaspoon basil
$1/2$ teaspoon rosemary
$1/2$ teaspoon salt
1 can tomato sauce
2 $1/2$ pounds zucchini thinly sliced

In a bowl, combine cream cheese, cottage cheese, sour cream, onion and green pepper. Brown ground beef with oregano, basil, rosemary and salt; stir in tomato sauce. In a 9" x 13" greased casserole, thinly layer a small amount of meat mixture; make a layer of zucchini, cover with a layer of cheese mixture. Repeat until all ingredients are used, ending with meat mixture. Cover and bake at 350 degrees for 30 minutes. Uncover and bake 30 minutes more.

"Great for those on low carb diet!"

Karyn Hobbs   **Lemoore High School, Lemoore, CA**

Main Dishes With **POULTRY**

Apple Chicken and Rice
Serves: 4 - 6

    1 pound boneless, skinless chicken breast, cut into 1" cubes
    2 tablespoons butter or margarine, divided
    1 package chicken flavor rice mix
    1 $1/4$ cups water
    1 cup apple juice
    1 to 2 (medium) apples, chopped
    1 cup fresh mushrooms, sliced
    $1/2$ cup onion, chopped
    $1/2$ cup Craisins

Brown chicken in large skillet in 1 tablespoon butter or margarine; remove and keep warm. In same skillet, saute rice (without seasoning packet) in remaining butter for 5 minutes. Add water and apple juice, apples, mushrooms, onions and contents of rice seasoning packet. Bring to a boil, reduce heat, cover and simmer 15 to 20 minutes. Add chicken, Craisins and a few apple slices for garnish; heat through.

"Uses less fat, sugar and salt."

Robin Ali　　　　　　　　　**Nevada Union High School, Grass Valley, CA**

Asian Chicken Wraps
Serves: 4　　　　　　　　　　*250 Cal; 6g Fat; 24g Carbs; 3g Fiber*

    1 teaspoon vegetable oil
    2 cups broccoli slaw (packaged, available in produce section)
    1 cup mushrooms, sliced
    $1/2$ pound chicken, cooked, diced
    $1/3$ cup chicken broth, low-sodium, lowfat
    $1/2$ teaspoon garlic
    dash salt
    1 tablespoon low-sodium soy sauce
    1 $1/2$ teaspoons cornstarch
    4 (6") flour tortillas

Main Dishes with Poultry

Heat oil over medium heat in large skillet. Add broccoli slaw and mushrooms; cook, stirring often, 3 to 4 minutes. Add chicken, broth, garlic, salt and pepper, stir. Cook, covered, over medium heat for 3 to 4 minutes. Combine cornstarch and soy sauce, stir until smooth. Add to skillet and stir constantly about 1 minute, until thickened. Spoon $1/4$ of chicken onto each tortilla and roll, like a burrito. Serve immediately.

"Great cold to take on a picnic or boating. Cut in half and wrap in foil. Low carb or fat free tortillas may be used to reduce carbs or fat even more."

Patty Bulat   **Rogers Middle School, Long Beach, CA**

Bacon Chicken
Serves: 8

8 strips bacon, partially cooked to remove the grease
8 boneless, skinless chicken breast halves
1 (small) jar dried beef, chopped
1 can cream of mushroom soup
2 cups sour cream
2 green onions, chopped
8 ounces mushrooms, sliced
1 tablespoon butter

Preheat oven to 275 degrees. Wrap partially cooked bacon around chicken breasts. Spread chipped beef on bottom of a baking pan. Top with chicken. Mix soup and sour cream together and pour over chicken. Bake, covered, 2 hours. Remove cover and continue cooking 1 hour more. During last 15 minutes of baking, saute green onion and mushrooms in butter. Garnish chicken with sauteéd mixture and serve.

"This is an old family recipe."

Jill Enright   **Granite Hills High School, El Cajon, CA**

Barbecued Chicken Quesadillas
Serves: 2

Nonstick cooking spray
2 (4 ounce) boneless, skinless chicken breasts
$1/4$ cup honey barbecue sauce
$1/2$ cup tomato, chopped
$1/4$ cup onion, chopped
2 tablespoons fresh cilantro, chopped
2 (8") flour tortillas
$1/4$ cup reduced fat sharp cheddar cheese, shredded

Preheat oven to 400 degrees. Place a medium nonstick skillet, coated with cooking spray over medium heat until hot. Add chicken and saute 6 minutes on each side. Remove from skillet; shred. Add barbecue sauce and toss. Combine tomato, onion and cilantro in a small bowl. Spoon half of the chicken mixture down the center of each tortilla. Top with tomato mixture and sprinkle with cheese. Fold over; secure with a wooden pick. Place on baking sheet. Bake 4 minutes or until cheese melts.

*"One of my favorite quick to fix recipes.
The sharp cheese gives a lot of flavor for a small amount!"*

Sue Hope   Lompoc High School, Lompoc, CA

Basil Chicken Vermicelli
Serves: 4

8 ounces dried vermicelli
1/3 cup sun-dried tomatoes, packed in oil, drained (reserve oil)
3 cloves garlic, minced
1 (medium) onion, chopped
2 (medium) zucchini, thinly sliced
1 bell pepper, diced
1 cup fat free, sodium-reduced chicken broth
2 cups cooked chicken, shredded
1/2 cup fresh basil, chopped or 3 tablespoons dried basil
Parmesan cheese, freshly grated

Bring 8 cups water to a boil in a 4 to 5 quart saucepan. Add pasta and cook 8 to 10 minutes or until al dente. Meanwhile, heat reserved oil from tomatoes in a wide nonstick frying pan. Sliver tomatoes, then add to fry pan along with garlic and onion, Saute a few minutes, then add zucchini and bell pepper. Cook, stirring often until vegetables begin to brown, 8 to 10 minutes. Pour broth over vegetables and bring to a boil. Drain pasta and add to vegetables with chicken and basil. Lift with 2 forks to mix. Transfer to a platter. Offer cheese to taste.

"Best if you use leftover grilled chicken breasts. A great summer meal!"

Patti Bartholomew   Casa Roble High School, Orangevale, CA

Caesar Chicken
Serves: 4

4 boneless, skinless chicken breasts
1 cup Marie's Caesar Salad Dressing
1/4 cup mayonnaise
1/2 cup Parmesan cheese, freshly grated
4 zucchini, shredded
1 tablespoon butter
1 clove garlic, minced

Preheat oven to 375 degrees. Place chicken in baking dish. Mix together salad dressing, mayonnaise and cheese. Spread evenly over chicken. Cover and bake 1/2 hour; uncover and bake 1/2 hour more. Saute shredded zucchini in butter and garlic until tender. Place mound of zucchini on plate, top with chicken breasts and drizzle sauce over all.

LaRae Harguess   **Hesperia High School, Hesperia, CA**

Chicken and Pasta with Salsa

Serves: 4   *408 Cal; 11g Fat; 50g Carbs; 2g Fiber; 30g Protein; 547mg Sodium; 118mg Chol*

1 (9 ounce) package refrigerated fresh angel hair or linguine pasta
3 broiled chicken breast halves
1 (16 ounce) La Victoria Salsa
1 tablespoon lime juice
$^1/_4$ cup Monterey Jack or Mozzarella cheese, shredded
Optional: Fresh cilantro or parsley sprigs

Prepare pasta according to package directions. Meanwhile, remove skin and bones from chicken breasts; cut meat into bite-sized strips. Stir together salsa, lime juice and chicken strips in large saucepan; heat through. Drain pasta and toss with salsa mixture. Sprinkle with cheese and garnish with cilantro or parsley sprigs.

"Quick and easy! '

Pat Smith   **Kern Valley High School, Lake Isabella, CA**

Chicken Asparagus Fajitas

Serves: 6   *350 Cal; 6g Fat; 46g Carbs; 5g Fiber; 23g Protein; 715mg Sodium; 45g Chol*

1 pound boneless, skinless chicken breasts. cut into strips
$^3/_4$ cup fat free Italian dressing
1 pound fresh asparagus, cut into 2" pieces
1 (medium) yellow pepper, sliced
1 (medium) red pepper, sliced
$^1/_2$ cup corn
$^1/_4$ cup onion, diced
2 tablespoons lemon juice
$^1/_2$ teaspoon garlic salt
$^1/_8$ teaspoon pepper
12 (7") flour tortillas, warmed

Toss chicken with dressing and refrigerate 4 hours, stirring several times. Drain and discard marinade. Saute chicken 3 minutes; add vegetables and cook, stirring for 7 minutes or until chicken is cooked and vegetables are tender-crisp. Stir in lemon juice, garlic salt, and pepper. Spoon $^1/_2$ cup filling onto each tortilla and serve.

"Fat is less because I cut out 1 tablespoon oil from the original recipe.
Also use low-fat tortillas. Original recipe came from Quick Cooking.*"*

Rulene Jeffs   **Kearns High School, Kearns, UT**

Chicken & Asparagus Roll-Up

Serves: 4   *Approx. 300 Cal; 15g Fat; 6g Carbs; 1g Fiber; 40g Protein*

    4 boneless skinless chicken breasts
    $1/2$ to 1 teaspoon Lawry's Seasoning Salt
    8 ounces Mozzarella or jack cheese, sliced
    20 pieces asparagus, cooked tender-crisp
    toothpicks
    1 tablespoon oil

Preheat oven to 350 degrees. Pound chicken breasts on cutting board until $1/2$" thick. Sprinkle with seasoning salt on both sides. Place $1/4$ of the cheese on each breast, leaving $1/2$" of chicken edge showing. Place 4 to 5 pieces asparagus on each breast. Cut off woody ends to fit chicken. Tightly roll up and secure with toothpicks. Heat oil over medium-high heat and brown chicken. Transfer to baking dish and bake for 15 to 20 minutes until juices run clear.

"Original recipe calls for Swiss cheese. Substitute any cheese you like!"
Julie Eyre   **Alhambra High School, Alhambra, CA**

Chicken Fajita Burritos

Serves: 4

    2 boneless, skinless chicken breasts
    $1/2$ cup Pace Picante Sauce
    1 tablespoon oil (optional)
    4 flour tortillas
    Toppings: Shredded lettuce; shredded cheese; picante sauce; sour cream

Cut chicken into bite-sized pieces. Cook in picante sauce and oil until mixture is dry. Wrap in flour tortillas or lettuce leaf with desired toppings.

"A student favorite. Easy and nutritious!
Students enjoy making this recipe for their families!"
Joyce Doig   **Ranchero Middle School, Hesperia, CA**

Chicken Fingers

Serves: 4   *230 Cal; 2g Fat; 31g Carbs; 1g Fiber; 19g Protein; 275mg Sodium; 45mg Cholesterol*

    12 ounces boneless, skinless chicken breasts
    2 egg whites
    1 tablespoon + $1/4$ cup honey, divided
    2 cups cornflakes, crushed
    $1/4$ teaspoon pepper
    4 teaspoons yellow or Dijon-style mustard
    $1/4$ teaspoon garlic powder

Preheat oven to 450 degrees. Rinse chicken; pat dry. Cut into 3" x $3/4$" strips. In a small bowl, combine egg whites and 1 tablespoon honey. In a shallow bowl, combine crushed cornflakes and pepper. Dip chicken strips into egg white mixture, then roll in crumb mixture to coat. Place in a single layer on ungreased baking sheet. Bake 11 to 13 minutes or until tender and no longer pink. Meanwhile, prepare a sauce by stirring together remaining $1/4$ cup honey, mustard and garlic powder. Serve with chicken.

"These are good for you! The honey-mustard dipping sauce is the perfect partner to these, a fat-skipping alternative to their fast food cousins."

Alice Claiborne   **Fairfield High School, Fairfield, CA**

Chicken, Mushroom & Broccoli Casserole

Serves: 4

4 boneless, skinless chicken breasts
1 can cream of mushroom soup
$1/2$ soup can water
$1/4$ cup mushrooms, sliced
2 cups broccoli florets

Wash and pat dry chicken breasts and place in casserole dish. Cover breasts with soup and $1/2$ can water. Add sliced mushrooms; cover and bake at 325 degrees for 1 $1/2$ hours. Add broccoli during last 45 minutes of baking.

"A tasty low-carb meal. You can serve over rice if you can afford the extra carbs and calories! You can also substitute other vegetables for the broccoli."

Linda Johnson   **Riverbank High School, Riverbank, CA**

Chicken Picante

Serves: 6   *194 Cal; 8g Fat; 329mg Sodium; 73mg Cholesterol*

$1/2$ cup medium to hot chunky taco sauce
$1/4$ cup Dijon mustard
2 tablespoons fresh lime juice
6 boneless skinless chicken breasts
2 tablespoons margarine
cilantro, chopped, for garnish
plain yogurt

Combine taco sauce, mustard and lime juice in large bowl. Add chicken, turning to coat. Cover; marinate in refrigerator at least 30 minutes. Melt butter in large skillet over medium heat until foamy. Remove chicken from marinade, reserving marinade. Add chicken to skillet and cook about 10 minutes or until browned on both sides. Stir in marinade and cook about 5 minutes or until chicken is tender and marinade glazes chicken. Remove chicken to serving platter. Boil marinade over high heat 1 minute; pour over chicken. Garnish with chopped cilantro and serve with yogurt.

Kathie Baczynski   **Mt. Carmel High School, Poway, CA**

Chicken Tacos

Serves: 4 - 5

> 4 to 5 boneless skinless chicken breasts
> 1 (28 ounce) can crushed tomatoes, with sauce
> 1 cup chicken broth
> $1/2$ teaspoon cumin
> $1/4$ teaspoon salt
> $1/4$ teaspoon pepper
> 12 corn tortillas
> $1/2$ cup oil, for frying
> *Toppings:* Chopped tomato, chopped cilantro, shredded lettuce, shredded cheese, sliced avocado, chopped onion, sour cream, salsa, etc.

Boil chicken until juices run clear. Remove chicken; chop or shred into bite-sized pieces. In medium saucepan, combine crushed tomatoes with chicken broth, cumin, chicken, salt and pepper; simmer 20 minutes. Fry corn tortillas in oil until crispy, folding in half as you fry. Drain on paper towels. Spoon chicken into tortillas, use your choice of topping.

"This is a family favorite. It is the first thing requested for family gatherings and birthdays. Don't fry the tortillas, just warm in the oven for a lighter meal."

Julie Eyre   **Alhambra High School, Alhambra, CA**

Chicken Vegetable Stir Fry

Serves: 4 - 6

> 2 tablespoons oil, divided
> 2 to 3 boneless, skinless chicken breasts
> $1/3$ cup water
> 1 tablespoon cornstarch
> $1/4$ cup soy sauce
> 1 tablespoon sugar
> $1/2$ onion, diced
> 2 stalks celery, chopped
> 2 carrots, sliced
> 1 stalk broccoli, chopped
> $1/2$ zucchini, chopped
> 5 mushrooms, sliced
> 2 to 3 cups rice, hot, cooked

Heat 1 tablespoon oil in frying pan. Add chicken and cook over medium heat until done; remove from skillet and set aside. In a small bowl, combine water and cornstarch. When cornstarch is dissolved, add

soy sauce and sugar; mix well and set aside. Heat remaining 1
tablespoon oil in skillet over medium heat. Add onion and cook until
translucent. Add celery and carrots; cook 3 minutes. Add broccoli and
zucchini; cook 2 minutes. Add mushrooms; cook 2 minutes more. Add
sauce mixture and cook 2 minutes more. When vegetables are cooked,
add cooked chicken and heat through. Serve over hot, cooked rice.

Dorene Bottis   **Alvarado Intermediate School, Rowland Heights, CA**

Chile Chicken Stack
Serves: 4

$^1/_2$ teaspoon vegetable oil
1 cup onion, chopped
2 cloves garlic, minced
1 cup chicken breast, chopped
salt and pepper, to taste
2 cups green chile sauce
nonstick cooking spray
6 corn tortillas
$^1/_2$ cup Monterey jack cheese, shredded

Preheat oven to 350 degrees. Heat oil in skillet over medium heat.
Saute onion and garlic until tender; add chicken, salt and pepper. Spread
$^1/_4$ cup green chile sauce on bottom of 11" x 7" baking pan that has been
coated with nonstick cooking spray. Lay 2 tortillas over bottom of pan.
Cover with half of the chicken mixture and $^1/_3$ cup chile sauce. Repeat
layers, ending with tortillas. Spread remaining sauce over tortillas;
sprinkle with cheese. Bake about 20 minutes or until heated through and
cheese has melted. Cut each tortilla stack in half. Serve.

"My kids really like this!"

April Rosendahl   **Chino High School, Chino, CA**

Citrus Chicken
Serves: 4   *400 Cal.*

4 boneless, skinless chicken breasts
1 egg
1 tablespoon water
2 slices whole grain bread
2 teaspoons lemon pepper
2 tablespoons canola oil
lemon slices
fresh parsley

Flatten chicken breasts with a mallet; set aside. Whip egg with water
in a small bowl; set aside. Pulse bread slices in a food processor until
coarse; add lemon pepper and pulse again. Turn out onto pie tin. Dip

chicken breasts into egg wash, then into seasoned bread crumbs. Heat oil in skillet over medium heat and fry chicken breasts, turning once, just until juices run clear. Serve with lemon slices and snipped fresh parsley.

"Serve with boiled, small red potatoes and a crisp green salad... satisfying"
Nancy Spillman   **Lucerne Valley High School, Lucerne Valley, CA**

Citrus Herb Roasted Chicken

Serves: 4   **For Chicken and skin: *239 Cal; 13.6g Fat; 27g Protein;***
Chicken without skin: *190 Cal; 7.4g Fat; 0 Carbs; 29g Protein*

1 whole chicken, washed, patted dry
salt and pepper
$1/2$ orange, sliced
$1/2$ lemon, sliced
4 cloves garlic
3 sprigs fresh thyme
3 sprigs fresh rosemary

Preheat oven to 425 degrees. Season chicken with salt and pepper, inside and out. Place chicken in roasting pan and stuff cavity with orange, lemon and 2 cloves garlic, 1 sprig thyme and 1 sprig rosemary. Tuck 1 clove garlic, 1 sprig thyme and 1 sprig rosemary in between each leg joint. Roast chicken in oven about 1 hour, or until thermometer inserted in thickest part of thigh registers 165 degrees. Let stand 10 minutes before carving.

"This is delicious and simple to prepare!"
Laura de la Motte   **Turlock High School, Turlock, CA**

Crockpot Chili

Serves: 6 - 8

2 pounds ground turkey
2 (16 ounce) cans red kidney beans, drained
2 (14.5 ounce) cans diced tomatoes
1 (large) golden onion, chopped
1 (large) green pepper, chopped
2 cloves garlic, minced
2 - 3 teaspoons chili powder
2 $1/2$ teaspoons salt
1 teaspoon pepper
white rice, cooked
cheddar cheese, shredded

Cook turkey in a large skillet until browned; drain. Combine turkey with next 8 ingredients in a crockpot and stir to mix well. Cover. Cook on low for 8 to 10 hours. Serve over white rice and top with shredded cheese.

"This lowfat version of chili is a nice alternative to using beef. You may want to adjust the seasonings to suit your taste."

Gerry Henderson   **Temple City High School, Temple City, CA**

Dash Diet Mexican Bake

Serves: 6   *304 Cal; 5.5g Fat; 38g Carbs; 7g Fiber; 31g Protein; 227mg Sodium*

1 $^1/_2$ cups cooked rice, preferably brown
1 pound boneless, skinless chicken breast, cut into bite-sized pieces
2 (14.5 ounce) cans no-salt added tomatoes, diced or crushed
1 (15 ounce) can no-salt added black beans, drained and rinsed
1 cup frozen yellow corn kernels
1 cup red bell pepper, chopped
1 cup poblano or green pepper, chopped
1 tablespoon chili powder
1 tablespoon cumin
4 cloves garlic, crushed
1 cup reduced fat Monterey Jack cheese, shredded
$^1/_4$ cup jalapeño pepper slices (optional)

Preheat oven to 400 degrees. Spread rice in shallow 3 quart casserole. Top with chicken. In a bowl, combine tomatoes, beans, corn, peppers, seasonings and garlic; pour over chicken. Top with cheese and jalapeño, if using. Bake 45 minutes.

"A heart healthy, easy to fix recipe that the whole family will find tasty!"

Mary Coffman   **Reed High School, Sparks, NV**

Easy Chicken in Wine Sauce

Serves: 4   *190 Cal; 15g Fat; 5g Carbs; 1g Fiber; 6g Protein; 117mg Sodium; 12mg Cholesterol*

4 tablespoons extra-virgin olive oil
1 clove garlic, crushed
3 boneless skinless chicken beasts, cut in strips
$^1/_8$ teaspoon salt
$^1/_4$ teaspoon coarsely ground black pepper
$^1/_2$ cup dry white wine
3 tomatoes, sliced

In a medium skillet, heat oil and garlic over medium heat. Sprinkle chicken with salt and pepper, then add to skillet and cook 7 to 10 minutes. Add the white wine and cook an additional 2 minutes. Remove chicken to a platter. Saute tomatoes in skillet until tender. Place tomatoes over chicken and cover with pan drippings.

"From the South Beach Diet Book. Quick and delicious!"

Myrna Swearingen   **Corona High School, Corona, CA**

Ellen's Honey Mustard Chicken

Serves: 4

4 to 6 boneless, skinless chicken breasts or skinless chicken parts
$1/2$ cup honey
$1/2$ cup yellow mustard
2 to 3 tablespoons lemon juice
dash garlic powder
sprinkle of paprika

Lay chicken breasts or pieces in baking pan. Mix honey, mustard and lemon juice. Pour mixture over chicken, cover and marinate at least 30 minutes. (Best if you can marinate several hours or overnight in refrigerator.) Sprinkle with paprika before baking. Bake at 350 degrees for 25 to 30 minutes until chicken is done.

"This is great! Low calorie and very tasty. Strip the chicken skin and fat off before marinating. Start this dish in the oven and finish on the grill for barbecue fans. Remember to boil any leftover marinade that you want to use as a sauce. Boil the sauce for 3 minutes or so to ward off salmonella bugs!"
Ellen Black-Eacker   **Nogales High School, La Puente, CA**

Garlic Teriyaki Chicken

Serves: 4

4 boneless skinless chicken breasts
1 cup teriyaki sauce
2 tablespoons soy sauce
2 tablespoons garlic, minced
1 tablespoon garlic powder
2 teaspoons pepper

In a bowl, combine all ingredients except chicken. Remove all fat from chicken breasts. Slice into strips. Marinate chicken strips in marinade for better flavor. Cook chicken in large skillet until done.

"Great to serve with white rice."
Christina Sargent   **Point Loma Nazarene University , San Diego, CA**

Gourmet Chicken Breasts

Serves: 4 - 6

4 chicken breasts, boneless, skinless
3 tablespoons butter
2 tablespoons oil
8 thin slices prosciutto
8 thin slices Fontina cheese
4 tablespoons Parmesan cheese, freshly grated
2 tablespoons chicken stock
salt and pepper, to taste

Preheat oven to 350 degrees. Slice each chicken breast to make 8 thin slices and pound each thin with a meat mallet. Brown each in the butter and oil, not crowding the pan. Do not overcook. Transfer chicken to baking dish. Place a slice of Prosciutto and Fontina on top of each breast. Sprinkle with grated Parmesan and dribble with chicken stock. Salt and pepper, to taste. Bake about 20 minutes or until cheese is melted and lightly browned.

"This dish should fit into most low-carb diets."

Lindy Cooper   **Simi Valley High School, Simi Valley, CA**

Greek Chicken

Serves: 2

2 (8 ounce) chicken breasts, boneless, skinless
2 to 3 lemons, squeezed
1 to 2 tablespoons Cavender's Greek Seasoning

Wash and remove all fat from chicken. Cut into strips or pieces. Squeeze lemon juice into a skillet and heat on low heat. When juice begins to bubble, add chicken and seasoning. Flip chicken over to cook until done. A lid may be added to steam in the flavor.

"Great to serve with couscous or a Greek salad."

Kristi Melton   **Marina High School, Huntington Beach, CA**

Green Enchilada Chicken Casserole

Serves: 6   *4.5 Carbs per serving*

4 cups chicken, cooked, cubed
2 teaspoons taco seasoning
8 ounces cream cheese, room temperature
1 (7 ounce) can Green Mexican sauce
1 (4 ounce) can chopped green chiles
6 ounces Monterey Jack cheese, shredded
4 green onions, chopped

Preheat oven to 350 degrees. Grease an 11" x 7" baking pan. Put chicken in pan and toss with taco seasoning to coat. In medium bowl, stir cream cheese and green sauce together; stir in chiles. Pour sauce evenly over chicken, top with cheese. Bake 25 minutes, until hot and bubbly, Remove from oven and immediately sprinkle with green onions.

"This recipe is easy and so good. It is a hit for dinner at my house."

Donna Baker   **Redlands East Valley High School, Redlands, CA**

Grilled Chicken & Nectarine Salad

Serves: 4   *260 Cal; 8g Fat; 68mg Chol*

4 chicken breasts, boneless, skinless
4 tablespoons lime juice, divided
2 tablespoons fresh thyme, chopped
  or 5 tablespoons dried thyme, divided
1 tablespoon + 1 teaspoon olive oil, divided
salt and pepper, to taste
1 (small) clove garlic, minced
5 nectarines, pitted, thinly sliced (about 2 cups)
6 cups mixed salad greens, torn
1 tablespoon pine nuts, toasted
$^1/_2$ cup fresh raspberries

Place chicken breasts in shallow dish. Sprinkle with 1 tablespoon lime juice, 1 tablespoon thyme and 1 teaspoon olive oil. Season with salt and pepper. Turn to coat. Cover and refrigerate 1 to 4 hours. Prepare grill and cook chicken until done, about 5 minutes per side. Cool. Cut chicken across grain in thin diagonal slices. Whisk remaining 3 tablespoons lime juice, 1 tablespoon thyme, 1 tablespoon olive oil and garlic in large bowl. Season with salt and pepper. Place nectarine slices in small bowl and add 1 tablespoon dressing; toss to coat. Add salad greens to remaining dressing; toss to coat. Divide salad greens amount 4 plates; arrange sliced chicken atop each serving. Top with nectarines. Sprinkle with pine nuts and garnish with raspberries.

"This is a gorgeous salad, a great low-calorie summertime meal."

Julie Shelburne   **Tulare Union High School, Tulare, CA**

Grilled Chicken with Fruit Salsa

Serves: 6   *257 Cal; 2.6g Fat; 16.7g Carbs; 2.7g Fiber; 40.9g Protein; 683mg Sodium 99mg Chol*

$1/_2$ cup lemon juice
$1/_2$ cup low-sodium soy sauce
1 tablespoon ginger, peeled, minced
1 tablespoon lemon pepper
2 cloves garlic, minced
6 (6 ounce) boneless skinless chicken breasts
1 $1/_2$ cups cubed pineapple
$3/_4$ cup kiwi fruit, peeled, cubed
$1/_2$ cup mango, peeled, chopped
$3/_4$ cup orange, peeled, coarsely chopped
$1/_2$ cup red onion, chopped
2 tablespoons cilantro, chopped
1 $1/_2$ teaspoons ground cumin
$1/_4$ teaspoon salt
$1/_8$ teaspoon pepper
1 (small) jalapeño pepper, seeded, chopped
nonstick cooking spray, for grilling

Prepare a marinade for chicken by combining lemon juice, soy sauce, ginger, lemon pepper and garlic in a large ziploc bag. Add chicken to bag; seal and shake to coat. Marinate in refrigerator 1 hour, turning once. Meanwhile, prepare salsa by combining fruit and remaining ingredients; toss gently. Prepare grill or broiler. Remove chicken from bag; discard marinade. Place chicken on grill or broiler pan coated with nonstick cooking spray. Cook 5 minutes on each side until done. Serve $1/_2$ cup salsa with each chicken breast.

"A great summer meal from Cooking Light."

Laurie Owen   **Challenger Middle School, San Diego, CA**

Healthy Chicken Taco Salad

Serves: 4

1 boneless skinless chicken breast, cubed
1 tablespoon oil
$1/_4$ cup salsa
1 $1/_2$ cups lowfat tortilla chips
1 $1/_2$ cups lettuce, shredded
$1/_2$ (15 ounce) can kidney beans, drained, rinsed
$1/_4$ cup tomato, chopped
$1/_2$ cup lowfat cheddar cheese, shredded
$1/_8$ cup green onions, diagonally sliced

Cook and stir chicken in oil over medium-high heat 4 to 5 minutes or until tender. Reduce heat to medium. Stir in salsa; cover. Simmer 5

minutes. Layer chips, lettuce, beans, chicken and tomato on serving
platter. Top with cheese and green onions.

Christine Katsilas   **Taylorsville High School, Taylorsville, UT**

Italian Style Turkey Cutlets

Serves: 1   *6 Carbs.*

    2 tablespoons Atkins Bake Mix
    salt and pepper, to taste
    1 turkey cutlet
    1 egg
    2 tablespoons olive oil
    2 slices roasted red bell pepper
    1 slice Mozzarella cheese
    fresh parsley, minced
    Optional toppings: Sautéed, sliced mushrooms;
       sauteéd diced eggplant; diced tomato, canned.

Preheat broiler. Season bake mix with salt and pepper. Dredge cutlet in
egg, then in bake mix. Saute cutlet in olive oil until nicely browned on
both sides. Place on foil-lined baking pan. Place pepper slices on top of
cutlet forming an "X" design. Top with cheese slice and broil until
cheese is melted. Sprinkle with parsley. Use optional toppings.

"You can substitute a butterflied chicken breast for the turkey cutlet.
Multiply the recipe by the number of cutlets you wish to serve."

Liz Coleman   **Oroville High School, Oroville, CA**

Lemon Linguine

Serves: 8

    1 pound linguine
    $1/2$ cup olive oil
    zest from 1 lemon
    juice from 2 lemons
    $1/2$ cup green onion, chopped
    $1/4$ cup fresh parsley, chopped
    salt and freshly ground pepper, to taste
    Parmesan cheese, freshly grated
    Additional: Chicken breast, cooked and chopped;
       $1/2$ cup pine nuts (optional)

Cook linguine in boiling salted water according to package directions,
until done; drain well. Combine next 5 ingredients in large serving bowl.
Add pasta and toss well. Sprinkle with salt and pepper. Toss in enough
Parmesan to suit your taste. Serve, or toss in additional ingredients of
your choice.

"This is a favorite dish hot or cold. Add additional ingredients for a main dish."

Kelly Smith   **Las Vegas High School, Las Vegas, NV**

Mesquite Chicken Kabobs Page 98

Southwest Citrus Chicken with Corn Salsa Page 103

Lowfat Chicken Caesar Salad

Serves: 3

2 chicken breasts
2 tablespoons olive oil
$1/_4$ teaspoon each salt, pepper, paprika
1 head Romaine lettuce, coarsely chopped
2 cloves garlic, minced
1 anchovy fillet, mashed, finely minced
pinch salt
juice of 1 lemon, seeded
3 drops Worcestershire sauce
$1/_2$ cup fat free, lowfat or light mayonnaise
2 to 3 tablespoons water
4 tablespoons Parmesan cheese, freshly grated, divided
$1/_2$ cup fat free croutons
1 cup cherry tomatoes
black pepper, coarsely ground, to taste

The day before or several hours before serving, roast chicken breasts in a baking pan along with olive oil, salt, pepper and paprika at 375 degrees until done, approximately 40 minutes, depending on size of chicken breasts. When cooled, cut into slices and chill. Wash, drain and pat dry lettuce leaves. Tear or cut into bite-sized pieces and chill. In a bowl, whisk together garlic, anchovy and salt until blended. Whisk in lemon juice, Worcestershire sauce, mayonnaise and water. When dressing is well combined and to the desired thickness you wish, whisk in 2 tablespoons of the Parmesan cheese. To assemble salad: Place lettuce in large salad bowl and toss with dressing until coated. Add croutons and toss. Divide salad between 3 plates. Top with tomatoes and sliced chicken. Sprinkle with remaining Parmesan cheese and serve.

"A great 2-hour lab activity and is our top sales item on our staff lunch menu."

Priscilla Burns　　　　　　　　　　**Pleasant Valley High School, Chico, CA**

Lowfat Tacos

Serves: 8

1 pound ground turkey
1 cup tomato sauce
1 teaspoon chili powder
$1/4$ teaspoon cumin
$1/8$ teaspoon oregano
$1/2$ cup water
4 to 5 (whole wheat, low carb) flour tortillas
1 cup lowfat Monterey jack cheese, grated
2 cups lettuce, shredded
$1/2$ tomato, chopped
bottled taco sauce

Spray a skillet with nonstick cooking spray. Cook turkey, mashing with a fork. Add the next 7 ingredients and simmer until thick. Spray an iron skillet with nonstick cooking spray. Warm tortillas on both sides until slightly hard. Place meat down center, add cheese, fold in half and heat until cheese melts. Remove from pan and add lettuce, tomato and taco sauce. Serve hot.

"Low carb tortillas are available. Students like the tacos.
We make these after the unit on fat and cholesterol."

Betty Plooy   **Vanden High School, Fairfield, CA**

Mesquite Chicken Kabobs

Serves: 4

1 cup Lawry's Mesquite Marinade with Lime Juice, divided
1 pound boneless, skinless chicken breasts, cut into chunks
1 (medium) red onion, cut into wedges
1 green bell pepper, cored, seeded, cut into 1" chunks
12 cherry tomatoes
12 mushrooms, cut in half
6 (8") skewers

Photo on page 4 and opposite page 96.

In large resealable plastic bag, combine $3/4$ cup Mesquite Marinade with Lime Juice and remaining ingredients, except skewers. Marinate in refrigerator 1 hour, turning occasionally, discard used marinade. On skewers, thread all ingredients. Grill or broil until chicken is thoroughly cooked, about 15 minutes; brushing often with remaining marinade.

"Wonderful for picnics and grill parties. For wrap sandwiches,
remove skewers after grilling and serve in flour tortillas."

Lawry's, Inc.   **Monrovia, CA**

Mexi Chili Mac

Serves: 4

1 pound ground turkey
$1/_2$ cup green bell pepper, chopped
$1/_4$ cup onion, chopped
1 clove garlic, crushed
1 (14.5 ounce) can Mexican style diced tomatoes, undrained
1 (8 ounce) can tomato sauce
$3/_4$ cup water
$3/_4$ cup uncooked elbow macaroni
2 teaspoons Spicy Seasoning Mix (see below)
$1/_2$ teaspoon salt
Spicy Seasoning Mix:
3 tablespoons chili powder
2 teaspoons ground cumin
1 $1/_2$ teaspoons garlic powder
$3/_4$ teaspoon dried oregano
$1/_2$ teaspoon ground red pepper

In a 3 quart saucepan, brown turkey with bell pepper, onion and garlic over medium heat 8 to 10 minutes or until turkey is no longer pink, breaking up into $3/_4$" crumbles. Pour off drippings. Stir in remaining ingredients. Bring to a boil; reduce heat to low. Cover tightly and simmer 15 minutes. Remove from heat; cover and let stand 5 minutes before serving. Note: To prepare seasoning mix, combine all ingredients. Cover and store in airtight container. Shake before using to blend.

"A California Beef Producer's recipe changed to use ground turkey. It is really easy because you cook the macaroni in the chili - only one pot to wash!"
Sandy Hughes   **Upland High School, Upland, CA**

Oriental Barbecued Chicken

Serves: 4   *305 Cal; 9g Fat; 49g Protein; 170mg Sodium; 135mg Chol.*

4 chicken breast halves, boneless, skinless
$1/_2$ cup hoison sauce
1 tablespoon sesame oil
1 tablespoon tomato paste
$1/_2$ teaspoon ground ginger
2 cloves garlic, crushed

Set oven control to broil. Trim fat from chicken breast halves. Place chicken on rack in broiler pan. Mix remaining ingredients together. Brush some sauce on chicken. Broil 7 to 8 minutes or until browned;

turn. Brush with sauce and broil 4 to 5 minutes longer or until juices of chicken run clear. Heat remaining sauce to boiling; serve with chicken.

"Recipe taken from one of my favorites Betty Crocker's Low-Fat, Low-Cholesterol Cookbook! *Not only healthy, but also quick and easy!"*

Melissa Webb   **Lakewood High School, Lakewood, CA**

Parmesan Chicken

Serves: 4   *160 Cal; 3g Fat*

$1/4$ cup Parmesan cheese, grated
2 tablespoons dried bread crumbs
1 teaspoon Italian seasoning
$1/8$ teaspoon paprika
4 boneless, skinless chicken breasts

Preheat oven to 400 degrees. In a small bowl, mix together Parmesan cheese, bread crumbs, Italian seasoning and paprika. Transfer mixture to a plate, dip each chicken breast in mixture coating all sides. Place on nonstick baking sheet. Bake 20 to 25 minutes.

"This is a family favorite. It's easy, low calorie and delicious!"

Cheri Schuette   **Valley View Middle School, Simi Valley, CA**

Philly Cheese Chicken Wrap

Serves: 4

4 chicken breasts, cubed
1 (medium) onion, chopped
1 green bell pepper, chopped
1 yellow bell pepper, chopped
1 red bell pepper, chopped
3 tablespoons margarine
salt and pepper, to taste
$1/3$ cup light sour cream
2 cups lowfat Monterey jack cheese, shredded
1 package low carb tortilla wraps

Saute onion and bell pepper in margarine until onion is transparent. Add chicken and brown. Salt and pepper, to taste. Remove about $1/4$ cup juice from pan and stir into sour cream (to avoid curdling). Stir back into pan and sprinkle cheese over top. Serve in a low carb wrap.

"You can also serve this over cooked broccoli."

Lori Wilson   **A.B. Miller High School, Fontana, CA**

Pineapple Chicken Stir-Fry

Serves: 2

$^1/_8$ cup soy sauce
1 tablespoon sugar
1 $^1/_2$ teaspoons vinegar
1 $^1/_2$ teaspoons catsup
$^1/_4$ teaspoon ground ginger
1 clove garlic, minced
1 chicken breast, cut into strips
1 tablespoon vegetable oil
$^1/_2$ package frozen stir-fry vegetables
1 cup pineapple chunks, unsweetened, drained
1 cup hot cooked rice

In a small bowl, combine first 6 ingredients; set aside. In a large skillet or wok, stir fry chicken in oil 5 to 6 minutes or until juices run clear. Add vegetables and stir fry 3 to 4 minutes or until tender-crisp. Stir in pineapple and reserved soy sauce mixture; heat through. Serve over hot cooked rice.

"This recipe incorporates many food groups for a healthy combination."
Gaylene Greenwood **Roy High School, Roy, UT**

Quick Southwest Chicken and Black Bean Skillet

Serves: 4

1 tablespoon olive oil
1 pound boneless skinless chicken breast, cut into 1" cubes
$^1/_2$ teaspoon dried thyme
$^2/_3$ cup salsa or picante sauce
$^3/_4$ cup instant brown rice
1 cup whole kernel corn
$^1/_3$ cup chicken broth
1 (15 ounce) can black beans, drained, rinsed
salt and pepper, to taste
cilantro or parsley, chopped (optional)

In a 12" nonstick skillet, over medium-high heat, combine oil, chicken and thyme. Cook, stirring 3 to 5 minutes or until chicken begins to brown. Stir in salsa; simmer 3 minutes. Add rice, corn, broth and beans. Simmer, covered 8 to 10 minutes, until chicken and rice are cooked through. Fluff and season with salt and pepper. Garnish with chopped cilantro or parsley and serve.

"Beans are a healthy food and black beans have great flavor. When added to recipes, brown rice does not change the flavor but it increases the nutrition."
Shauna Young **Jordan High School, Sandy, UT**

Salsa Chicken

Serves: 2

2 boneless skinless chicken breasts
Italian dressing (any brand)
2 tomatoes, diced
$1/4$ onion, diced
$1/4$ cup cilantro, chopped

Heat oven to 325 degrees. Place chicken breasts in baking pan and pour Italian dressing over, to coat. Bake 20 minutes. Meanwhile, mix tomatoes with onion and cilantro; set aside. When chicken is done, top with tomato salsa and serve.

"Add a vegetable or salad and your dinner is complete!"

Angela Brown   **Sonora High School, Sonora, CA**

Santa Fe Chicken

Serves: 4   *212 Cal; 4.4g Fat; 13g Carbs; 9g Fiber; 30g Protein; 72mg Chol*

juice of 3 limes
$1/4$ cup low-sodium soy sauce
1 $1/2$ teaspoons olive oil
1 $1/2$ teaspoons chili powder
1 $1/2$ teaspoons cumin seed
6 cloves garlic, minced
1 $1/2$ teaspoons honey
2 whole chicken breasts, boneless skinless
$1/4$ cup white wine
3 tablespoons cilantro, chopped
Garnish: salsa, sour cream and lime

Mix together first 7 ingredients in a bowl, stirring thoroughly. Lay chicken in a shallow baking dish. Pour marinade over chicken; cover and refrigerate for 1 hour. Preheat broiler. After chicken has marinated, pour in white wine. Broil chicken under a medium flame 8 to 10 minutes, basting with juices to keep it moist. Transfer chicken to platter and slice at an angle. Garnish if desired.

Lori Luna   **Lemoore High School, Lemoore, CA**

Southwest Citrus Chicken with Corn Salsa

Serves: 6

1 (12 ounce) bottle Lawry's Herb & Garlic Marinade with Lemon Juice
$1/_2$ cup orange juice
$1/_2$ cup fresh cilantro, chopped
1 $1/_2$ teaspoons Lawry's Lemon Pepper
1 $1/_2$ teaspoons Lawry's Seasoned Salt, divided
1 teaspoon crushed red pepper flakes
6 boneless, skinless chicken breasts
3 (large) ears fresh corn, shucked
2 tablespoons Bertolli Olive Oil
1 (large) tomato, diced
$1/_2$ cup red onion, diced
$1/_2$ cup green bell pepper, diced

> Photo
> opposite
> page 96

In large resealable plastic bag, mix together first 6 ingredients; reserve $2/_3$ cup of marinade mixture. Add chicken to bag; seal and marinate in refrigerator at least 30 minutes. Meanwhile, brush corn with olive oil. Grill over medium heat until browned, about 8 minutes, turning occasionally; cool. Carefully remove corn kernels using sharp knife (about 2 cups). In medium bowl, combine corn, last 3 ingredients, $1/_2$ teaspoon Seasoned Salt and $1/_3$ cup reserved marinade mixture; set aside. Remove chicken from bag; discard used marinade. Grill chicken over medium heat, brushing with remaining reserved marinade mixture, until chicken is thoroughly cooked, about 15 minutes. To serve, top chicken with corn salsa.

Lawry's, Inc.   **Monrovia, CA**

Southwestern Chicken Salad

Serves: 4 - 6

> Photo
> opposite
> page 33

1 (1.27 ounce) Lawry's Fajitas Spices & Seasonings
3 tablespoons vegetable oil
2 $1/_2$ tablespoons lime juice
1 $1/_2$ teaspoons Lawry's Garlic Powder with Parsley
6 boneless, skinless chicken breasts, (about 1 $1/_2$ pounds)
6 cups lettuce, torn
$1/_2$ red onion, thinly sliced
1 (large) tomato, cut into wedges
1 avocado, peeled, seeded, thinly sliced
Ranch style dressing

In small bowl, mix together Fajitas Spices & Seasonings, oil, lime juice and Garlic Powder with Parsley. In large resealable plastic bag, add chicken and marinade mixture; seal bag and toss to coat chicken. Refrigerate 30 minutes or overnight. Remove chicken from bag, discarding marinade. Grill or broil until chicken is thoroughly cooked, about 10 to 15 minutes. Let cool slightly, slice thinly or cut into cubes. To arrange salads, place chicken on beds of lettuce. Top each with equal portions of onion, tomato and avocado. Drizzle with ranch dressing.

"A perfect main dish salad served just with warm, crusty bread or cornbread!"
Lawry's, Inc.   **Monrovia, CA**

Stuffed Chicken Parmigiana

Serves: 6

> 6 to 8 boneless, skinless chicken breasts
> 2 cups hazelnut meal
> 1 egg
> 1 (16 ounce) container ricotta cheese
> 1 (3 ounce) container Kraft Romano cheese
> 1 1/2 cups Kraft Parmesan cheese, grated
> 1/2 teaspoon dried basil
> 1 teaspoon dried oregano
> 1 jar Paul Newman's Marinara Style Sauce
> 1/4 cup butter
> 1/4 cup Crisco or shortening
> Freshly grated Parmesan cheese, for topping

Slit chicken breasts lengthwise, to make pocket. Combine ricotta, Romano and Parmesan, basil, thyme, and oregano in a mixing bowl; it will be crumbly. Stuff mixture into pockets of chicken, leaving a small edge to seal. Using non-colored toothpicks, sew edges closed. Line a baking sheet with aluminum foil and melt butter and Crisco in oven at 350 degrees for about 5 minutes. Brush chicken with egg and dredge in hazelnut meal, coating well; place on baking sheet. Bake at 400 degrees for 15 minutes. Turn chicken and bake 15 to 20 minutes more. While chicken is baking, heat pasta sauce until hot. Remove chicken from oven, remove toothpicks and spoon pasta sauce over each breast. Top with freshly grated Parmesan cheese, if desired.

"Hazelnut meal can be purchased at Trader Joe's and in some grocery stores. It significantly lowers the carb count in this dish."

Beckie Bloemker   **Foothill High School, Sacramento, CA**

Swiss Chicken Cutlets

Serves: 4   *223 Cal; 7g Fat; 4g Carbs; 32g Protein; 178mg Sodium; 84mg Chol.*

2 (thin) slices reduced fat Swiss cheese, about 2 ounces
4 boneless, skinless chicken breasts, pounded with a mallet to flatten
2 tablespoons flour
$1/2$ teaspoon black pepper
1 tablespoon butter or margarine
$1/2$ cup lowfat chicken broth
$1/4$ cup dry white wine or lowfat chicken broth
$1/4$ teaspoon dried oregano
fresh parsley, for garnish

Cut each cheese slice in half; place one half on top of each chicken breast. Starting with short end, tightly roll up chicken breasts, jelly-roll style. Tie securely with string. On waxed paper, combine flour and pepper; mix well. Add chicken, tossing gently to coat. In large nonstick skillet, melt butter over medium heat. Add chicken and cook, turning frequently until golden brown, about 5 to 10 minutes. Add broth, wine and dried oregano to skillet. Increase heat; bring to a boil. Reduce heat to medium-low and simmer until chicken is cooked through and sauce is slightly thickened. Turn chicken over a few times to keep moist, 10 to 12 minutes. Place on a serving plate; remove string. Garnish with parsley.

"I serve this with wild rice, spinach salad, steamed vegetables and fresh fruit for dessert."

Marianne Traw   **Ball Junior High School, Anaheim, CA**

Turkey Sloppy Joes

Serves: 6

1 onion, minced
1 clove garlic, minced
1 green pepper, seeded, chopped
1 tablespoon oil
1 pound ground turkey
$1/2$ cup water
1 (8 ounce) can tomato sauce
$1/2$ teaspoon salt
1 teaspoon cornstarch
$1/4$ teaspoon dry mustard
$1/4$ teaspoon celery seed
$1/2$ teaspoon chili powder
6 hamburger buns, toasted

Saute onion, garlic and green pepper in oil in a medium skillet over medium-high heat. Cook until vegetables are soft. Remove vegetables from pan and use the same pan to brown ground turkey. Drain any grease. Return vegetables to pan. Add water, tomato sauce and all spices.

Bring to a boil. Reduce heat and simmer 10 minutes, stirring occasionally. Serve over toasted hamburger buns.

"This is great recipe that everyone (especially children) enjoy!"

Debby Truitt   **Woodland High School, Woodland, CA**

Turkey Veggie Meatballs

Serves: 4

> 1 $1/_2$ pounds ground turkey
> $1/_2$ cup dry bread crumbs
> $1/_2$ cup Parmesan cheese, grated
> $1/_3$ cup green onion, chopped
> $1/_4$ cup carrot, shredded
> $1/_4$ cup zucchini, shredded
> $1/_4$ cup fresh parsley, chopped
> $1/_4$ teaspoon salt
> $1/_4$ teaspoon pepper
> 1 egg white
> 2 cloves garlic, crushed
> 2 tablespoons flour
> 1 can beef broth
> $1/_2$ cup cream

Combine ground turkey with bread crumbs, cheese, vegetables, salt, pepper, egg white and garlic. Form into 1 $1/_2$" balls. Brown in hot skillet that has been sprayed with nonstick cooking spray. Set aside. Blend flour with cold beef broth until flour is dissolved. Heat, stirring constantly, until thickened. Add cream and stir until heated through. Add cooked meatballs and serve over hot, cooked rice or noodles.

"A look at the ingredients is a clue to the lowfat yummy quick entreé."

Linda Hsieh   **Rowland High School, Rowland Heights, CA**

Turkey with Black Bean Salsa

Serves: 3 - 4

1 teaspoon garlic salt
$1/2$ teaspoon ground cumin
$1/4$ teaspoon paprika
1 package turkey breast tenderloins
1 (15 ounce) can black beans, rinsed, drained
1 (large) tomato, chopped
1 tablespoon diced chiles, drained
2 to 3 tablespoons salsa
2 tablespoons fresh cilantro or parsley, chopped
2 tablespoons fresh lime juice
3 tablespoons, 1 teaspoon olive oil, divided
$1/8$ teaspoon salt
$1/4$ cup red onion, finely chopped

In a small 9" x 9" x 2" pan, mix garlic salt, cumin and paprika; add turkey and coat all sides. Refrigerate at least 30 minutes. In small bowl, mix beans, tomatoes, chiles, salsa, cilantro, lime juice, 2 teaspoons olive oil and salt. Cover and refrigerate until serving time. Rub turkey with 2 tablespoons olive oil and grill or saute in large skillet, heat 2 teaspoons olive oil over medium heat; cook turkey 7 to 10 minutes on each side, until no longer pink inside. Serve with black bean salsa.

"This is quick, easy and healthy. Serve with warm tortillas."

Rebecca Bolt   **Bear Creek High School, Stockton, CA**

Main Dishes With PORK

5 Spice Grilled Pork with Sweet & Sour Orange Glaze

Serves: 4

1 $1/2$ teaspoons chili powder
1 teaspoon sugar
$1/2$ teaspoon salt
$1/4$ teaspoon 5 Spice Powder
1 pork tenderloin
$1/2$ cup orange marmalade
2 tablespoons fresh lime juice
1 teaspoon green onion, finely chopped

Prepare grill for medium-hot fire. Blend chili powder, sugar, salt and 5 spice powder together in a small bowl. Rub mixture all over tenderloin and allow to blend during preparation time. In a small saucepan, bring marmalade, lime juice and green onion to a boil for about 2 minutes. Allow to cool and transfer half of the mixture to a small bowl. (Reserve the remaining half for serving.) Grill tenderloin until well done, 20 to 25 minutes, or until a meat thermometer reads 160 degrees. Turn and brush with half of the glaze while grilling. When tenderloin is done, wrap in foil to rest before serving. Warm remaining glaze and drizzle over sliced pork tenderloin.

Barbara Allen   **Ayala High School, Chino Hills, CA**

Deep Dish Quiche Pizza
Serves: 6

1 (4 ounce) package cream cheese
4 eggs
$1/3$ cup heavy cream
$1/4$ cup Parmesan cheese, freshly grated
1 tablespoon chives, chopped
$1/2$ teaspoon Italian seasoning
2 cups Italian cheeses, shredded
$1/4$ teaspoon garlic powder
$1/2$ cup low carbo-licious pizza sauce
1 cup Mozzarella cheese, shredded
Toppings: Pepperoni, ham or bacon bits, browned ground beef or turkey,
   black olives, mushrooms, chopped green pepper and onion

Preheat oven to 375 degrees. Beat together cream cheese and eggs
until smooth. Add cream, Parmesan cheese and spices and mix again.
Spray 9" or larger glass baking dish with nonstick cooking spray.
Sprinkle 2 cups Italian cheese into dish and pour in egg mixture. Bake
30 minutes. Remove from oven and let stand 5 minutes. Spread pizza
sauce over top and sprinkle with Mozzarella cheese. Pile high with your
desired toppings. Return to oven and bake until bubbly and browning.
Allow to stand 10 to 15 minutes before cutting.

"A low carb alternative to traditional pizza!
Only 5 carbs per serving without toppings."

Diana Lee   **David A. Brown Middle School, Wildomar, CA**

Pork Tenderloin with Orange Marmalade
Serves: 4   *160 Cal; 3g Fat; 175mg Sodium; 74mg Cholesterol*

1 (1 pound) pork tenderloin
1 $1/2$ tablespoons coarse grain mustard
1 to 2 cloves garlic, minced
$1/2$ teaspoon fresh rosemary, finely chopped
$1/4$ teaspoon fresh ground black pepper
$1/4$ cup low-sugar orange marmalade
$1/2$ cup water
2 (5" to 6") rosemary branches
$1/4$ cup chicken stock

Preheat oven to 400 degrees. Make a cut lengthwise down center about
halfway through the pork tenderloin. In a small bowl, mix mustard,
garlic, rosemary and black pepper. Spread mixture along the cut surface
of tenderloin. Reshape and tie in several places. Place a rack above
roasting pan. Brush with 2 tablespoons marmalade. Add water and
rosemary branches to the roasting pan. Bake 40 to 45 minutes or until an

internal temperature reaches 160 degrees. Mix together remaining orange marmalade and chicken stock in a small saucepan. Simmer 2 to 3 minutes until thickened. Spoon sauce over sliced tenderloin and serve immediately.

"Family favorite adapted from The T-Factor Diet. I hope you enjoy it!"
DeeAnn Verdi   **North Valleys High School, Reno, NV**

Spicy Pork Chops
Serves: 4   *273 Cal; 11g Fat; 21g Carbs; 1g Fiber; 22g Protein; 241mg Sodium; 63mg Chol*

4 boneless pork loin chops, about $1/2$" thick
1 (6 ounce) can vegetable juice cocktail
2 tablespoons green onion, sliced
2 tablespoons diced green chiles
1 clove garlic, minced
1 teaspoon Worcestershire sauce
$1/2$ teaspoon dried basil, crushed
few dashes bottled hot pepper sauce
2 cups hot cooked orzo or rice

Trim fat from pork chops. Combine vegetable juice cocktail, green onion, chiles, garlic, Worcestershire, basil and hot pepper sauce. Put chops in shallow bowl. Pour juice mixture over meat; cover and chill 2 to 24 hours, turning occasionally. Drain chops, reserving marinade. Place chops on unheated rack of a broiler pan. Broil 3" to 4" from heat for 4 minutes. Turn and broil 4 to 5 minutes or until juices run clear. In a small saucepan, heat reserved marinade to a full boil. Serve hot marinade with pork chops and hot orzo or rice.

"This is a main dish that can be mixed in advance
and then prepared in about 10 minutes."
Charlotte Runyan   **Saddleback High School, Santa Ana, CA**

Main Dishes
With SEAFOOD

Cilantro Salmon Bake

Serves: 1

    nonstick cooking spray
    5 ounces salmon fillet
    2 tablespoons fresh ginger, chopped
    $1/2$ cup scallions, chopped
    $1/4$ cup cilantro, chopped
    2 teaspoons soy sauce

Preheat oven to 350 degrees. Spray a 9" x 9" baking dish with nonstick cooking spray. Place salmon fillet in bottom of dish. Sprinkle with ginger, scallions, cilantro and soy sauce. Cover tightly with foil and bake 20 minutes. (This can also be wrapped in foil and cooked on the barbecue grill.) Note: Skip the ginger and soy sauce and use cilantro, lemon pepper and fresh lime juice!

> *"I really like salmon and cilantro and this makes a good combination! Salmon is low carb and high protein!"*

Camille Hicks   **Riverton High School, Riverton, UT**

Grilled Sea Bass

Serves: 4   *349 Cal; 18.5g Fat; 1.2g Carbs; 0.1g Fiber; 42.2g Protein; 243mg Sodium*

    $1/4$ teaspoon garlic powder
    $1/4$ teaspoon onion powder
    $1/4$ teaspoon paprika
    lemon pepper, to taste
    sea salt, to taste
    2 pounds sea bass, halibut or sole
    3 tablespoons butter
    2 (large) cloves garlic, chopped
    1 tablespoon fresh parsley, chopped
    1 $1/2$ tablespoons extra virgin olive oil

Preheat an outdoor grill for high heat and lightly oil grate. In a medium bowl, blend garlic powder, onion powder, paprika, lemon pepper and sea salt. Place sea bass in the bowl and rub to coat with seasonings. In a small saucepan over medium heat; mix butter, garlic and parsley. Remove from heat when butter has melted and set aside. Place sea bass on the prepared grill. Cook approximately 7 minutes. Flip and drizzle with the butter mixture. Continue cooking about 7 minutes, until easily flaked with a fork. Drizzle with olive oil before serving.

"This is a truly flavorful dish that is pretty on a plate. My mom and I experimented and made this for lunch. It came out so well I promptly went to the fish market so I could make it for my dinner guests that night."

Stephanie San Sebastian　　　　　　　　　**Central High School, Fresno, CA**

Halibut Mexican-Style

Serves: 3

> 1 pound halibut fillets, frozen
> 2 tablespoons Soy Garden Trans-Fat Free Spread
>   or butter or margarine, melted
> 1/2 teaspoon salt
> 1 (8 ounce) jar salsa
> 1 (small) can black or green olives, sliced
> lemon wedges

Preheat oven to 450 degrees. Put fillets on a piece of oven foil and seal edges. Place on cookie sheet and bake 25 minutes. Turn back foil and pour melted spread, butter or margarine over fish. Sprinkle with salt and top with salsa and olives. Bake, uncovered, until sauce is hot, about 10 minutes. Serve with lemon wedges.

"One of Nanci Morris' great Alaska halibut recipes!"

Mary Springhorn　　　　　　　　　**Anderson High School, Anderson, CA**

Halibut with Relish

Serves: 4

> 3 tablespoons olive oil
> 1 1/2 cups red and green bell pepper, chopped
> 1/2 cup red onion, chopped
> 3 cloves garlic, chopped
> 1/2 teaspoon dried thyme
> 1/2 cup pimiento stuffed green olives, chopped
> 2 tablespoons balsamic vinegar
> 1 tablespoon tomato paste
> dash cayenne pepper
> 4 (8 ounce) halibut fillets, broiled

Heat oil over medium-high heat and saute peppers, onion and garlic until soft. Add additional ingredients (except fillets) and heat through. Serve on top of broiled cooked halibut.

"Yummmmmmmm!"

Kris Hawkins   **Clovis West High School, Fresno, CA**

Honey Glazed Salmon

Serves: 4   *360 Cal; 16g Fat; 20g Carbs; 35g Protein; 1170mg Sodium*

nonstick cooking spray
4 tablespoons honey
4 tablespoons soy sauce
3 tablespoons fresh lime juice
1 tablespoon Dijon-style mustard
2 tablespoons water
1 tablespoon vegetable oil
1 1/2 pounds salmon fillets, cut into 4 pieces

Whisk together honey, soy sauce, lime juice, mustard and water; set aside. Heat oil in nonstick 12' fry pan over medium-high heat. Add salmon and cook 3 minutes on each side or until golden brown and just cooked. Transfer salmon to platter. Add honey mixture to pan and simmer 2 minutes. Pour over salmon and serve.

Betty Wells   **Bidwell Junior High School, Oroville, CA**

One Pot Dinner - Shrimp

Serves: 2

2 (6 ounce) cans shrimp, drained
1 (4 ounce) can stewed tomatoes
1 stalk celery, chopped
1 green pepper, chopped
1 bay leaf
1/4 teaspoon cayenne pepper

Heat all ingredients together over medium heat. Serve.

Julia Lane-Hiltz   **Durango High School, Las Vegas, NV**

One Pot Dinner - Tuna

Serves: 2

1 (6 ounce) can tuna, drained
3 tablespoons dry milk
1 (4 ounce) can peas
1 tablespoon onion flakes
1 (14 ounce) can mushrooms, drained, liquid reserved
salt and pepper, to taste
1 can French-style green beans

In saucepan, heat tuna with dry milk, peas, onion flakes, mushrooms and $1/4$ cup liquid reserved from mushrooms. Salt and pepper, to taste. Serve over heated green beans.

Julia Lane-Hiltz   **Durango High School, Las Vegas, NV**

Pan Fried Catfish

Serves: 4 - 6

> 4 - 6 fish fillets (catfish, red snapper, etc.)
> 1 egg beaten
> 2 tablespoons water
> $1/3$ cup bread crumbs
> 1 teaspoon salt
> $1/2$ teaspoon pepper
> 1 teaspoon Italian seasoning
> 1 teaspoon cayenne pepper
> oil, enough to cover bottom of pan

Rinse fish fillets with cold water and pat dry. Beat egg and water together. Mix all dry ingredients together. Dip fillets in egg wash and the lay them in the bread crumb mixture to completely coat. Heat oil to medium-high. Fry until golden and fish is flaky.

"You can add other seasonings to the bread crumb mixture. My students enjoy preparing and eating the fish. Several of them had never eaten catfish!"

Roberta Marshall   **Deer Valley High School, Antioch, CA**

Pasta & Garlic-Lemon Tuna Sauce

Serves: 5   *114 Cal.; 10g Fat; 1g Carbs.; 475 mg. Sodium; 6 mg. Chol..*

> 3 tablespoons olive oil
> 6 (medium) cloves garlic, minced or pressed
> $1/2$ teaspoon red pepper flakes
> 3 tablespoons capers, rinsed and drained
> $1/2$ cup dry white wine
> 2 cans solid white tuna, in water, drained well
> 1 teaspoon salt, or as needed
> $1/4$ cup fresh parsley leaves, chopped
> 1 teaspoon zest from 1 lemon, grated
> 1 tablespoon unsalted butter, cut into small pieces
> 1 pound whole wheat penne or fusilli, cooked al dente and drained
> $1/4$ cup pasta cooking water (reserve)
> ground black pepper, to taste

Heat oil, 1 tablespoon garlic, red pepper flakes and capers in 12" skillet over medium-high heat, stirring frequently, until fragrant and sizzling, but not browned, 1 to 2 minutes. Add wine and bring to simmer. Simmer until aroma bears no trace of alcohol, about 1 minute. Add tuna and salt; cook, stirring frequently until tuna is heated through, about 1 minute. Toss tuna mixture, remaining garlic, parsley, lemon zest, butter, cooked pasta and reserved pasta water to coat in warm serving bowl. Season with salt, pepper and lemon juice to taste; serve quickly.

"Uses many healthful foods like tuna, garlic, parsley, and whole wheat pasta."
Sonja Erickson   **Maria Carrillo High School, Santa Rosa, CA**

Salmon on the Grill

Serves: 8 - 10   *No Carbs!*

> 2 salmon fillets
> 2 tablespoons butter
> 1 (small) onion, sliced paper thin
> 2 lemons, thinly sliced
> Montreal Steak Seasoning

Cut 4 large pieces of foil; layer two together making two piles. Spray with nonstick cooking spray and lay 1 fillet on each pile of foil. Roll foil edges to make a canoe around fillet. Place several small dabs of butter on each fillet. Continue with onion and lemon slices. Sprinkle lightly with Montreal Steak Seasoning. Place on a low-heat gas grill for 20 to 30 minutes. Cut fillets into serving pieces or place whole fillets on a lettuce-lined platter.

Gail McAuley   **Lincoln High School, Stockton, CA**

Salmon Steaks with Grilled Red Onion Slices

Serves: 4

> 4 (6 ounce) salmon steaks or fillets
> 1 red onion, peeled, thickly sliced
> $1/4$ cup teriyaki sauce
> 2 tablespoons vinegar
> 4 cloves garlic, minced
> 1 teaspoon dried ginger
> 1 teaspoon sesame oil

Rinse fish thoroughly and place in a glass dish; top with onion slices. Combine teriyaki sauce, vinegar, garlic, ginger and oil. Pour over salmon and onion slices. Marinate 15 to 30 minutes. Remove from marinade and place on a greased grill rack. Grill over hot fire for 10 minutes per inch of thickness of fish.

"Salmon has high levels of Omega-3, the fatty acid that lowers blood pressure, lessens the risk of heart disease, and helps prevent certain types of cancer."
Sue Hope   **Lompoc High School, Lompoc, CA**

Scallops & Bell Peppers over Whole Wheat Linguine

Serves: 3 Zone Diet: Balanced Carbs-Protein-Fat

2 teaspoons butter
2 teaspoons canola oil
1 red bell pepper, julienned
1 clove garlic, chopped
13 ounces scallops
$1/4$ cup lowfat milk
pepper, to taste
3 cups hot, cooked whole-wheat linguine
$1/2$ cup fresh parsley, chopped

In a large skillet, melt butter and oil over medium heat. Add bell pepper and garlic; saute 2 minutes, stirring continuously. Add scallops, cover for 1 minute, turn scallops and saute for 1 minute more. Reduce heat to medium-low; add milk and pepper. Cook until scallops appear opaque. Toss the pasta with scallops and parsley; serve.

"Scallops are quick, easy and a healthy source of protein. They are my new personal favorite!"

Val Poalillo   **Paso Robles High School, Paso Robles, CA**

Seafood Enchiladas

Makes: 10   *241 Cal; 11g Fat; 19g Carbs; .4g Fiber; 17g Protein; 334mg Sodium*

Filling:
2 to 3 dried ancho chili peppers
2 cups jack cheese, shredded
12 ounces shrimp, cooked, chopped
10 (6") corn tortillas
Sauce:
$1/2$ cup onion, chopped
1 tablespoon olive oil
$1/3$ cup all-purpose flour
$1/4$ teaspoon salt
$1/4$ teaspoon ground black pepper
3 cups milk

Filling: Cut peppers open; discard stems and seeds. Cut into small pieces and place in small bowl. Cover with boiling water and let stand 60 minutes to soften; drain well. In a medium bowl, combine 1 $1/2$ cups cheese, shrimp and pepper pieces; set aside. Wrap tortillas tightly in foil. Heat in 350 degree oven for about 10 minutes. Spoon about $1/4$ cup filling on each tortilla near end; roll up. Place filled tortillas, seam side down, in a 2 quart oblong baking dish.

Sauce: In a medium saucepan, cook onion in hot oil until tender. Stir in flour, salt and pepper. Add milk all at once; cook and stir until thick and bubbly. Pour sauce over tortillas. Bake, covered, in a 350 degree oven about 20 minutes or until heated through. Remove foil and sprinkle with remaining cheese. Return to oven and bake 5 minutes more, until cheese melts.

"My family loves these enchiladas, and they are low in calories too!"

Charlotte Runyan   **Saddleback High School, Santa Ana, CA**

Teriyaki Salmon with Fresh Pineapple Salsa

Serves: 4

1 $1/_4$ pounds fresh salmon fillets or steaks

1 cup + 1 $1/_2$ tablespoons Lawry's Teriyaki Marinade
  with Pineapple Juice, divided

1 cup fresh or canned pineapple ($1/_2$" pieces), well drained

$1/_4$ cup red onion, diced into $1/_4$" pieces

1 tablespoon fresh cilantro, chopped

2 tablespoons red bell pepper, diced into $1/_4$' pieces

1 tablespoon fresh jalapeño chile, minced

> Photo
> opposite
> page 97

In resealable plastic bag, combine 1 cup Teriyaki Marinade with Pineapple Juice and salmon. Marinate in refrigerator 30 minutes or up to several hours. In small bowl, lightly mix 1 $1/_2$ tablespoons Teriyaki Marinade, pineapple, onion, cilantro, red bell pepper and jalapeño chile. Let pineapple salsa stand at room temperature up to 1 hour. Grill salmon on both sides over high heat about 5 to 6 minutes per side, brushing with additional marinade, if desired. To serve, top with salsa.

Lawry's, Inc.   **Monrovia, CA**

Teriyaki Salmon

Serves: 4 - 6

1 (1 to 2 pound) whole salmon fillet
1 1/2 cups light soy sauce
1/4 cup sake
1/2 cup brown sugar
2 tablespoons ground ginger
8 cloves garlic, minced

Combine all ingredients for marinade in the morning or night before. Let stand in the refrigerator for at least 4 hours. Begin marinating fish only 2 to 3 hours before dinner, depending on thickness of fillet. Grill, skin side first, on medium-high heat. Turn only once, about 7 minutes per inch of thickness of fillet or until only slightly rare. Fish should be moist. It if is dry or flakes easily, it has been overcooked.

"My husband developed this recipe and it has become one of our family's favorites. It's low in fat and high in Omega oils which help fight heart disease."

Delaine Smith   **West Valley High School, Cottonwood, CA**

Main Dishes Without MEAT

10-Minute Chili

Serves: 4

> 1 (15 ounce) can kidney beans, drained, rinsed
> 2 cups fat free spaghetti sauce
> 2 teaspoons chili powder
> 1 teaspoon ground cumin
> dash cayenne pepper (optional)

Place all ingredients in a saucepan and heat for 10 minutes, stirring occasionally. Ladle into bowls and serve.

"Serve with baked tortilla chips."

Michelle Rutherford   **California State University , Fresno, CA**

Hearty Multi-Bean Chili

Serves: 6

> 1 tablespoon oil
> 1 (medium) onion, chopped
> 1 carrot, chopped
> 1/2 bell pepper, chopped
> 2 cloves garlic, minced
> 1 (28 ounce) can tomatoes, diced
> 1 (15 ounce) can kidney beans, drained, rinsed
> 1 (15 ounce) can pinto beans, drained, rinsed
> 1 (15 ounce) can black beans, drained, rinsed
> 1 (8 ounce) can tomato sauce
> 1 tablespoon sugar
> 2 tablespoons chili powder
> 2 teaspoons cumin

Heat oil in Dutch oven over medium heat. Add onion, carrots, bell pepper, garlic; stir and cook 4 minutes. Add remaining ingredients and mix well. Bring to a boil. Reduce heat; cover and simmer 30 to 40 minutes. Serve with shredded cheddar cheese on top.

"This is a great veggie chili!"

Debbie Harvey   **Amador Valley High School, Pleasanton, CA**

Lowfat Stuffed Shells

Serves: 4 - 6

> 2 quarts water
> $1/_2$ teaspoon salt
> 16 to 20 jumbo shells
> 1 cup fat free ricotta cheese
> $1/_4$ cup fat free cottage cheese
> $1/_2$ cup lowfat Mozzarella cheese, shredded
> 3 tablespoons Parmesan cheese, grated
> 2 egg whites
> 1 teaspoon parsley
> $1/_4$ teaspoon oregano
> 2 green onions, finely chopped
> dash salt and pepper
> 1 $1/_2$ cups fat free spaghetti sauce
> Parmesan cheese, freshly grated, for garnish.

In large saucepan, bring water and salt to a boil. Add jumbo shells, 3 or 4 at a time, until all are in the pot. Boil, uncovered for 10 minutes, stirring occasionally. (Avoid overcooking.) Drain and cool on waxed paper or parchment paper, keeping them separated so they don't stick together. While shells are cooking, mix together ricotta cheese, cottage cheese, Mozzarella, Parmesan, egg whites, parsley, oregano, green onion, salt and pepper. Fill each shell with about 2 to 3 tablespoons of cheese mixture. Spread a thin layer of spaghetti sauce on bottom of a glass casserole dish. Place shells, open side down, in dish and cover with remaining sauce. Cover with foil. Bake at 350 degrees for about 35 to 40 minutes or until hot and bubbly. Place shells, open end down, onto plate and garnish with freshly grated Parmesan cheese.

Christine Katsilas   **Taylorsville High School, Taylorsville, UT**

Mexican Black Bean Chili

Serves: 6 1-1/3 cup servings   *362 Cal; 4.4g Fat; 19.5g Carbs; 14g Fiber*

2 (15 ounce) cans black beans
2 cups onion, chopped
1 cup yellow bell pepper, chopped
1 cup red bell pepper, chopped
1 cup green bell pepper, chopped
1 tablespoon chili powder
2 teaspoons cumin seeds
2 teaspoons dried oregano
1 teaspoon salt
$1/2$ teaspoon ground cinnamon
1 (15 ounce) can Italian-style tomatoes, undrained, chopped
1 $1/2$ ounces semi-sweet chocolate, coarsely chopped
4 cloves garlic, minced
2 jalapeño peppers, seeded, chopped
2 bay leaves
1 cup fresh cilantro, minced
1 to 2 teaspoons hot sauce

Drain and rinse beans. Put beans and next 14 ingredients in a slow cooker. Cover with lid and cook on low for 8 hours. Stir in cilantro and hot sauce. Colorful, nutritious and absolutely delicious!

"Know what low-carb means! Refined sugar and processed Carbs should be kept low in the diet - the majority of one's diet still needs to come from carbohydrates. They need to be whole grain, high fiber, non-refined Carbs!"

Dale Sheehan   **Santana High School, Santee, CA**

Mushroom Lasagna

Serves: 8

9 spinach or regular lasagna noodles, uncooked
$1/4$ cup butter or margarine
1 pound fresh mushrooms, sliced (6 cups)
2 cloves garlic, minced
$1/2$ teaspoon salt
1 teaspoon lemon juice
$1/4$ cup flour
3 cups milk
$1/2$ cup fresh parsley, chopped
1 (15 ounce) carton ricotta cheese
8 ounces Mozzarella cheese, shredded
$1/2$ cup Parmesan cheese, grated

Cook lasagna noodles as directed on package; drain and rinse with hot water. In large saucepan, melt butter or margarine. Add mushrooms, garlic, salt and lemon juice; saute until tender, about 5 minutes. Stir in flour; blend well. Add milk. Cook over medium-high heat until mixture thickens and boils, stirring constantly, Stir in $^1/_3$ cup parsley. Heat oven to 325 degrees. To assemble, spread $^1/_2$ cup sauce in ungreased 9" x 13" baking dish. Layer $^1/_3$ of the noodles, $^1/_3$ ricotta, $^1/_3$ Mozzarella, $^1/_3$ remaining sauce and $^1/_3$ Parmesan; repeat layers until ending with Parmesan cheese on top. Bake 45 minutes or until bubbly. Let stand 10 to 15 minutes before serving.

"To make lower in fat, replace milk with skim milk and regular ricotta with lowfat or nonfat ricotta. My husband is a big meat eater but loves this recipe."

Betty Rabin-Fung   **Sierra Vista Junior High School, Canyon Country, CA**

Peggy's Garden Fettuccini
Serves: 4 - 6   *509 Cal.*

    12 ounces dried fettuccini
    3 cups (small) fresh broccoli florets
    1 cup light sour cream
    $^3/_4$ cup Parmesan cheese, grated
    $^1/_3$ cup cherry tomatoes, halved

Cook pasta according to package directions. About 3 minutes before pasta is done, add broccoli florets and continue cooking. Remove from heat. Ladle out 3 cups pasta cooking liquid and reserve. Drain pasta and broccoli. Mix sour cream, Parmesan cheese and cooking liquid. Mix together all ingredients and toss well.

Angela Croce   **Mira Mesa High School, San Diego, CA**

Spinach & Mushroom Frittata
Serves: 4   *Low Carbs*

    4 teaspoons olive oil
    $^1/_2$ cup onion, chopped
    12 mushrooms, sliced
    8 ounces spinach, chopped
    2 whole eggs
    6 egg whites
    salt and pepper, to taste
    $^1/_2$ teaspoon oregano
    4 ounces feta cheese, crumbled

Preheat oven to 375 degrees. In an ovenproof skillet, heat olive oil and saute onion, mushrooms and spinach. Meanwhile, beat whole eggs and egg whites with salt, pepper, oregano and feta; set aside. Drain spinach mixture and add to egg mixture, then return to skillet. Bake in oven for 30 to 40 minutes or until fully set.

Eleni Karapoulios   **Cypress High School, Cypress, CA**

Sweet Yellow Peppers & Tomatoes with Feta Cheese

Serves: 6   *69 Cal; 3.2g Fat; 9.1g Carbs; 2.2g Fiber; 2.4g Protein; 147mg Sodium; 6mg Chol.*

3 tablespoons red wine vinegar
1 tablespoon water
1 1/2 teaspoons olive oil
3/4 teaspoon dried oregano
1/2 teaspoon Dijon mustard
1/8 teaspoon salt
1 clove garlic, minced
3/4 cup red onion, thinly sliced
6 plum tomatoes, cut lengthwise into 1/8" thick slices
2 yellow bell peppers, cut into 1/8" thick rings
1/4 cup feta cheese, crumbled
freshly ground pepper

Combine first 7 ingredients in a small bowl, stirring well with a whisk. Combine 1 tablespoon vinegar mixture and onion in a small bowl, tossing well. Spoon onion mixture evenly onto a serving platter. Arrange tomato around edge of platter; place pepper rings in center of platter on top of onion. Drizzle remaining vinegar mixture over vegetables. Top with cheese and sprinkle with black pepper.

"A colorful low-calorie salad with lots of flavor!"

Sue Hope   **Lompoc High School, Lompoc, CA**

Tomato Basil Pasta

Serves: 6

1/2 pound capellini pasta
1/2 cup olive oil
2 cloves garlic, minced
5 (large) Roma tomatoes, seeded, chopped
2 tablespoons fresh basil, chopped
1 teaspoon salt
1/4 teaspoon coarse black pepper
Parmesan cheese, grated

Prepare pasta according to package directions; drain. In a large skillet, heat oil. Stir fry garlic 1 minute (do not brown). Add tomatoes, basil, salt and pepper; stir and cook 2 minutes. Toss tomato mixture with hot pasta. Serve on warm platter. Sprinkle with Parmesan cheese.

Beverly Ranger   **Carpinteria High School, Carpinteria, CA**

Vegan Veggie Rice Bowl

Serves: 6

$1/4$ bunch broccoli, chopped
1 carrot, peeled, cut into match stick pieces
2 green onions, sliced
4 mushrooms, sliced
$1/2$ cup pea pods
$1/4$ cup beans sprouts
$1/2$ cup water
$1/4$ cup soy sauce
2 teaspoons cornstarch
1 clove garlic
$1/4$ teaspoon ginger
2 tablespoons oil
4 ounces tofu, cut into cubes

Wash and prepare vegetables. Combine water, soy sauce, cornstarch, garlic and ginger to make sauce. Heat oil in large skillet. Add onions, broccoli, carrots and cook until tender. Add remaining vegetables and cook until tender. Add tofu and stir until warm and coated with sauce. Serve over rice.

"This is the old vegetarian stir fry updated for 2004."

Debbie Harvey   **Amador Valley High School, Pleasanton, CA**

Vegetable Quiche

Serves: 4 - 6

1 (9") pie crust
1 cup lowfat Swiss Cheese, shredded
2 cups assorted vegetables, chopped
  (mushrooms, zucchini, broccoli, cauliflower)
6 egg whites or $3/4$ cup egg substitute
1 cup nonfat milk
$1/4$ cup Parmesan cheese, grated

Preheat oven to 350 degrees. Bake pie crust 5 to 6 minutes. Cool 5 minutes. Put Swiss cheese and vegetables on bottom of crust. In a separate bowl, beat egg whites and milk together. Pour mixture over vegetables. Sprinkle with Parmesan cheese. Bake 35 to 40 minutes or until firm.

"My mom and sister take this dish to many luncheons and get rave reviews!"

Diane Castro   **Temecula Valley High School, Temecula, CA**

Vegetable Pizza with Fantastic Pizza Crust

Serves: 12

Crust:
1 cup water, very warm
1 tablespoon yeast
1 teaspoon sugar
1 teaspoon salt
3 tablespoons oil
   (olive, peanut, safflower, sunflower, corn or soybean oil)
2 1/2 cups whole wheat flour
nonstick cooking spray

Topping:
2 (8 ounce) packages fat free cream cheese
2/3 cup fat free mayonnaise
1 tablespoon dill weed
1 tablespoon onion powder
6 green onions, sliced
2 carrots, finely grated
2 green peppers, finely chopped
6 radishes, sliced
3 tomatoes, diced
2 cups broccoli florets
2 cups cauliflower florets
1 can pineapple tidbits, drained

Preheat oven to 450 degrees. Combine water, yeast, sugar, salt, oil and flour. (Dough must be stiff so it can be worked with easily.) Spread evenly on pizza pan that has been coated with nonstick cooking spray. Bake 8 to 13 minutes; remove from oven and cool. Mix together cream cheese, mayonnaise, dill weed and onion powder. Spread mixture over top of baked pizza crust. Top with veggies and pineapple. Serve cold.

"Makes a sumptuous summer time or any time meal."

Linda Stokes   **Riverton High School, Riverton, UT**

Cakes Cookies & DESSERTS

Almond Cookies

Makes: 2 1/2 dozen   *1g Fat*

    2 $^1/_2$ cups flour
    1 cup sugar
    1 cup butter, softened
    $^1/_8$ teaspoon salt
    $^1/_2$ teaspoon baking soda
    $^1/_2$ cup egg substitute
    1 tablespoon almond extract

Preheat oven to 325 degrees. Mix flour, sugar, butter, salt and baking soda. Add egg substitute and almond extract. Drop by spoonfuls onto a greased baking sheet. Bake 20 to 23 minutes.

"Only 1 fat gram per cookie!"

Natalie Henwood   **Riverton High School, Riverton, UT**

Almond Joy Pie

Serves: 8   *7 Carbs per serving*

    Crust:
    1 cup almond flour
    2 tablespoons Splenda
    3 tablespoons butter
    $^1/_4$ teaspoon coconut extract
    Filling:
    1 package sugar free chocolate pudding
    1 $^1/_2$ cups heavy cream
    $^1/_2$ cup water
    Topping:
    1 cup heavy cream
    2 tablespoons Splenda
    $^1/_4$ teaspoon coconut extract
    1 to 2 tablespoons unsweetened coconut
    1 to 2 tablespoons almonds, chopped
    chocolate shavings, from low-carb chocolate bar

Preheat oven to 400 degrees. Lightly butter a 9" pie pan. Melt butter in small bowl. Mix almond flour and sugar substitute together and add to melted butter. Stir in extract and mix well. Press mixture into pie pan, over bottom and up sides. Bake about 10 minutes, until golden brown, checking frequently so it doesn't burn. Cool crust and put in freezer while you prepare filling. In a medium bowl, place sugar free pudding mix, heavy cream and water. Beat with electric mixer until you get a thick mousse-like consistency. Spread this into cooled crust. Prepare topping: In medium bowl, place heavy cream, Splenda and coconut extract. Beat with electric mixer until soft peaks form. Spread over filling. Sprinkle pie with shredded coconut, chopped almonds and chocolate shavings. Refrigerate 4 hours before serving.

"Heavenly! My absolute favorite low-carb dessert... my family loves it too!"

Donna Baker   **Redlands East Valley High School, Redlands, CA**

Angel Food DeLight

Serves: 12   *No fat, low sugar*

    1 (large) package raspberry sugar-free gelatin
    2 (small) packages frozen, sugar free strawberries, thawed
    1 (large) angel food cake
    3 (large) bananas
    1 (large) fat free Cool Whip

Prepare gelatin using package directions. Stir in strawberries and refrigerate until soft set. Slice cake lengthwise, 3 times. Using a 9" x 13" x 2" pan, layer 1 slice cake, $1/3$ gelatin, 1 sliced banana, $1/3$ Cool Whip; repeat 2 more times, ending with Cool Whip. Chill 1 to 2 hours. Slice and serve.

Paula Schaefer   **Garside Junior High School, Las Vegas, NV**

Angel Food Pineapple Cake

Serves: 8 - 12

    1 box angel food cake mix
    1 (20 ounce) can crushed pineapple

Preheat oven to 350 degrees. Mix cake mix with pineapple until well blended. Bake in a 9" x 13" or bundt pan, 40 to 45 minutes. Serve plain, topped with fresh fruit or Cool Whip.

"Light and easy. I got this from a Weight Watchers meeting."

Libby Newman   **West Valley High School, Hemet, CA**

Apple Crumble

Serves: 8   *250 Cal.*

  6 Granny Smith apples, peeled, cored, sliced
  $1/2$ cup raisins (optional)
  $1/4$ cup walnut or pecans (optional)
  $3/4$ cup sugar
  $1/4$ cup lemon juice
  $1/2$ teaspoon cinnamon
  $1/8$ teaspoon allspice
  1 teaspoon all-purpose flour
  nonstick cooking spray
  1 $1/2$ cups granola

Preheat oven to 350 degrees. In a large bowl, toss apples, raisins, nuts, sugar, lemon juice, cinnamon, allspice and flour. Lightly spray a Pyrex pan with nonstick cooking spray and place mixture into pan. Sprinkle granola on top of mixture and cover with foil. Bake, covered, for 1 hour; remove foil and bake until crumble is lightly browned. Allow to set 15 to 20 minutes before serving.

"Easy to make, tastes great! Class will enjoy making it on first day and eating on the second."

Eleni Karapoulios   **Cypress High School, Cypress, CA**

Banana Pudding

Serves: 10   *359 Cal.*

  $1/3$ cup all-purpose flour
  dash salt
  2 $1/2$ cups 1% lowfat milk
  1 (14 ounce) can fat free sweetened condensed milk
  2 egg yolks
  2 teaspoons vanilla extract
  3 cups ripe bananas, peeled, sliced
  45 reduced fat vanilla wafers
  4 egg whites
  $1/4$ cup sugar

Preheat oven to 325 degrees. Combine flour and salt in medium saucepan; gradually stir in milk, condensed milk, and egg yolks. Cook over medium heat, stirring constantly, 8 minutes or until thickened. Remove from heat and stir in vanilla. Arrange 1 cup banana slices in a 2 quart baking dish. Spoon $1/3$ pudding mixture over bananas; top with 15 vanilla wafers. Repeat layers once. Top with remaining bananas and pudding. Arrange remaining 15 vanilla wafers around inside edge of dish. Gently push wafers into pudding. In separate bowl, beat egg whites at high speed with an electric mixer until foamy. Add sugar, 1

Chocolate Bits Cheesecake **Page 130**

Chocolate Cream Brownie Torte **Page 131**

Silky Chocolate Mousse **Page 143**

tablespoon at a time, beating until stiff peaks form and sugar dissolves (2 to 4 minutes). Spread meringue over pudding, sealing to edge of dish. Bake for 25 minutes or until golden. Let cool at least 30 minutes.

"Friends and family will love this lighter version of a classic family favorite!"

Judy Dobkins   **Redlands High School, Redlands, CA**

Café Latté Custard

Serves: 6

> 1 (12 ounce) can nonfat evaporated milk
> 3 to 4 tablespoons instant espresso coffee
> $^1/_2$ cup sugar
> 1 cup nonfat milk
> $^3/_4$ cup egg substitute
> 2 teaspoons vanilla
> $^1/_4$ teaspoon almond extract
> few coffee beans, crushed

Preheat oven to 350 degrees. Heat evaporated milk, espresso and sugar until dissolved; remove from heat. Stir in nonfat milk, egg substitute and flavorings. Divide mixture between 6 custard cups; place into a hot water bath and bake 15 to 20 minutes, until a knife inserted in center comes out clean. Chill and garnish with crushed coffee beans.

"From a dear friend who had to change her whole diet after extensive bypass surgery. She has given me some excellent recipes. This one is very good!"

Sandra Massey   **Mt. View High School, El Monte, CA**

Cheesecake Cupcakes

Serves: 8 - 10   *4g Carbs per average serving*

> 1 package unflavored gelatin
> 1 cup boiling water
> 2 (8 ounce) packages cream cheese, softened
> 1 teaspoon vanilla
> 10 packages artificial sweetener (equal to $^1/_2$ cup sugar)
> 1 to 2 cups low-carb fruit preserves

Line 18 to 24 muffin cups with cupcake liners. Dissolve gelatin in the boiling water in a mixing bowl, stirring well. Cut cream cheese into small pieces and place in dissolved gelatin. Add the vanilla and sweetener and beat well with electric mixer. Pour into prepared muffin cups. Chill until firm, about 2 hours. Top each cupcake with $^1/_2$ teaspoon preserves.

Diana Lee   **David A. Brown Middle School, Wildomar, CA**

Cheesecake Pudding

Serves: 4   130 Cal.

2 cups fat free plain yogurt
1 cup crushed pineapple (do not drain)
1 (small) box sugar free, fat free vanilla instant pudding

In a bowl, mix all ingredients together. Spoon into half cup serving
glasses. Chill.

"When my daughter, Stephanie, was young,
she loved to make this dessert for our family. It's delicious!"

Cheri Schuette   **Valley View Middle School, Simi Valley, CA**

Chocolate Bits Cheesecake

Serves: 12   370 Cal; 25g Fat; 17g Carbs; 6g Fiber; 21g Protein; 390mg Sodium; 120mg Chol

2 cups lower carbohydrate crunchy almond crisp cereal
$1/_4$ cup butter or margarine, melted
4 (1.1 ounce) bars Hershey's 1 Gram Sugar Carb Chocolate Candy
3 (8 ounce) packages Neufchatel cheese
   ($1/_3$ less fat cream cheese), softened
1 cup Splenda
$1/_4$ cup nonfat dry milk powder
3 eggs
1 (8 ounce) container dairy sour cream
2 teaspoons vanilla

Photo
opposite
page 128

Prepare crumb crust: Heat oven to 350 degrees. Crush cereal to make
1 cup crumbs; stir together with melted butter and press onto bottom and
$1/_2$" up side of a 9" springform pan. Bake 8 to 10 minutes; cool. Remove
wrappers from candies, chop into $1/_4$" pieces and set aside. Beat cream
cheese, Splenda and milk powder until smooth. Add eggs, one at a time,
beating well after each addition. Blend in sour cream and vanilla. Set
aside two tablespoons of chopped chocolate pieces; stir remaining into
cheesecake batter. Pour batter into prepared crust. Bake 35 to 40 minutes
or until almost set. Remove from oven to wire rack. With knife, loosen
cake from side of pan. Cool completely; remove sides of pan. Place
remaining 2 tablespoons candy pieces in small microwave-safe dish;
microwave on HIGH 30 seconds; stir. If necessary, microwave on HIGH
15 seconds at a time; stirring after each heating, until chocolate is
melted and smooth when stirred. Drizzle chocolate over cheesecake
surface. Cover, refrigerate several hours or until chilled. Garnish as
desired. Cover and refrigerate leftovers.

Hershey Kitchens   **Hershey, PA**

Chocolate Cream Brownie Torte

Serves: 12   *360 Cal; 32g Fat; 15g Carbs; 4g Fiber; 5g Protein; 240mg Sodium; 140mg Chol*

1 1/4 cups butter
3/4 cup Hershey's Dutch Processed Cocoa
1 cup + 2 tablespoons Splenda
3 tablespoons all-purpose flour
4 eggs, separated
2 teaspoons vanilla
1 tablespoon granulated sugar
4 (1.1 ounce) bars Hershey's 1 Gram Sugar Crab Chocolate Candy
1 (8 ounce) package cream cheese, softened
1 cup Splenda
1 cup frozen non-dairy whipped topping, thawed

Photo
opposite
page 128

Heat oven to 350 degrees. Grease bottom of 9" springform pan. Melt butter over low heat; stir in cocoa. Remove from heat and cool, about 5 minutes. Stir together Splenda and flour; blend into cocoa mixture. Add egg yolks, one at a time, beating well after each addition. Stir in vanilla. Beat egg whites with granulated sugar until soft peaks form, gradually fold into chocolate mixture. Spread batter into prepared pan. Bake 15 to 18 minutes, or until edges are firm (center will be slightly soft). Cool completely. Prepare chocolate cream: Remove wrappers from candy; break into pieces. Place in small microwave-safe bowl and microwave on HIGH 30 seconds; stir. If necessary, microwave on HIGH 15 seconds at a time, stirring after each heating, until chocolate is melted and smooth when stirred. Beat cream cheese and Splenda in medium bowl until well blended. Beat in melted chocolate; blend in whipped topping. Spread over surface of torte. Refrigerate several hours or until thoroughly chilled. Garnish as desired. Cover and refrigerate leftovers.

Hershey Kitchens   **Hershey, PA**

Chocolate-Orange Hazelnut Biscotti

Makes: 40   *54 Cal; 11g Carbs; 1g Fat; 1g Protein; 34mg Sodium; 11mg Chol*

1/4 cup hazelnuts, shelled
2 1/2 cups all-purpose flour
1/4 cup unsweetened cocoa powder
3/4 teaspoon baking soda
1/4 teaspoon salt
1 cup sugar
2 (large) eggs
1 (large) egg white
1 1/2 teaspoons orange zest, grated
1 teaspoon vanilla

Preheat oven to 350 degrees. Spray a baking sheet with nonstick cooking spray; set aside. Place hazelnuts in a baking pan and toast 8 to 10 minutes, or until skins loosen and nuts are lightly browned. Place in a kitchen towel and rub to remove skins. Finely chop the nuts; set aside. Reduce oven temperature to 325 degrees. In a large bowl, combine flour, cocoa, baking soda and salt; set aside. In another bowl, with an electric mixer at medium speed, beat the sugar, eggs, egg white, orange zest and vanilla until well combined. With mixer at low speed, gradually add dry ingredients and hazelnuts and beat until well combined. Turn dough onto a lightly floured surface. Shape dough into two 12" long logs. Place the logs on the prepared baking sheet and bake 20 to 25 minutes or until bottoms are lightly browned and tops are set. Remove logs to a wire rack to cool for about 10 minutes. Cut each log diagonally into $1/2$" thick slices. Return the slices to the baking sheet and bake another 10 to 15 minutes, (turning Biscotti once halfway through baking) or until lightly toasted over all. Transfer to wire racks to cool completely.

"The word Biscotti means twice baked, and these Italian specialities do go into the oven twice. The dough, formed into a log, is baked until firm, and then the logs are sliced and re-baked to produce crisp cookies that are traditionally served with a beverage for dunking."

Ruth Schletewitz   **Rafer Johnson Junior High School, Kingsburg, CA**

Cinnamon Sugar Cookie Twists
Makes: 12 - 15

    1 package Pillsbury Frozen Puff Pastry Dough (2 sheets)
    4 tablespoons water
    1 to 2 eggs
    cinnamon-sugar mixture

Thaw pastry dough according to package directions. Roll one sheet of pastry to 12" x 9". Cut the dough into 2 pieces that measure 6" x 9" each. Mix egg and water to make an egg wash. Brush egg wash on one side of each 6" x 9" piece of dough. Sprinkle cinnamon-sugar mixture over one piece of dough until saturated. Place the second piece of dough (egg wash side down) on top of the cinnamon-sugared piece to make a sandwich. Cut sandwich into $1/2$" x 1" x 6" pieces. Grease a cookie sheet (or use parchment paper). Twist strips before placing them on sheet. Brush twists with egg wash. Bake 10 to 15 minutes at 400 degrees. Remove twists from oven and place on paper towels to cool.

Carol Kagy   **Norwalk High School, Norwalk, CA**

Debbie's Sugar-Free Apple Pie

Serves: 6 - 8

> pastry for double-crust pie
> 5 crisp baking apples, sliced thin (I like Pippin)
> $1/2$ cup apple juice, frozen
> $1/4$ cup flour
> $1/4$ cup + 3 tablespoons butter, divided
> $1/2$ teaspoon cinnamon
> $1/2$ teaspoon nutmeg

Place 1 crust in bottom of pie plate; set aside. Preheat oven to 425 degrees. Slice apples; set aside. Mix together frozen apple juice, flour, $1/4$ cup butter, cinnamon and nutmeg, then stir in sliced apples. Pour into unbaked pie shell. Dot top of apples with remaining 3 tablespoons butter before putting on top crust. Seal edges with fork. Put slits on top of crust. Bake 40 to 50 minutes.

"I developed this recipe for my brother who cannot eat sugar.
It is now his favorite dessert. We prefer this over a regular pie recipe."

Debbie Farr   **Foothill High School, Santa Ana, CA**

Fancy Frozen Fruit Cups

Serves: 18

> 2 cups water
> $3/4$ cup sugar
> $3/4$ cup orange juice concentrate
> $3/4$ cup lemonade concentrate
> 1 (20 ounce) can pineapple tidbits, drained
> 2 (medium) firm bananas, cut into $1/2$" slices
> 1 $1/2$ cups watermelon chunks
> 1 $1/2$ cups green grapes
> 1 $1/2$ cups strawberries, quartered
> 1 $1/2$ cups peaches, cubed
> 2 kiwi fruit, peeled, quartered, sliced

In a small saucepan, bring water and sugar to a boil, stirring constantly. Remove from heat. Stir in juice concentrates. In a large bowl, combine all the fruit except kiwi. Add juice mixture and mix well. Place about $1/2$ cup fruit mixture in 5 ounce disposable wine glasses or 5 ounce cups. Top each with 4 kiwi pieces. Cover and freeze until firm. Remove from freezer about 1 $3/4$ hours before serving.

"These are great to make in the summer and keep in the freezer
for a quick snack or dessert."

Carole Delap   **Golden West High School, Visalia, CA**

Floating Fruit Parfait

Serves: 6   **50 Cal; 2g Fat; 6g Carbs**

$1/_2$ cup strawberries, sliced
$3/_4$ cup boiling water
1 (4 serving) package Jello brand Strawberry Flavor Sugar Free Gelatin
$1/_2$ cup cold water
$3/_4$ cup ice cubes
1 $1/_2$ cups Cool Whip Lite

Divide fruit among 6 parfait glasses. Stir boiling water into gelatin until dissolved. Stir in cold water and ice cubes until ice melts. Pour $3/_4$ cup gelatin over berries in glasses. Refrigerate 20 minutes or until set, but not firm. Stir 1 cup whipped topping into remaining gelatin with wire whisk until smooth. Spoon over gelatin in glasses. Refrigerate 1 hour. Garnish with remaining topping.

"I got this recipe from Jello.com and really like serving it in the summer, using various fresh fruits of the season."

Joanne Montoy   **Esperanza High School, Anaheim, CA**

French Silk Pie

Serves: 8   **1.5g Carbs**

1 $1/_2$ cups nuts, ground
$3/_4$ cup + 3 tablespoons Splenda, divided
$1/_2$ cup +2 tablespoons butter, softened, divided
2 squares unsweetened baking chocolate
1 teaspoon vanilla
2 eggs
1 pint heavy cream

Heat oven to 400 degrees. Combine ground nuts with 3 tablespoons Splenda and 2 tablespoons butter; press into a 9" pie plate and bake 6 to 8 minutes; cool. Cream remaining $1/_2$ cup butter with $3/_4$ cup Splenda. Melt chocolate and blend into mixture when cooled. Stir in vanilla. Add eggs, one at a time. With electric mixer, beat 5 minutes after adding each egg. Don't skimp on the beating time. Pour into prepared crust. Chill 1 to 2 hours, minimum. Whip heavy cream, adding just enough Splenda to desired sweetness. Top pie with whipped cream and serve.

"You might feel like you're cheating, but you're not!"

Cathy Miller   **Montclair High School, Montclair, CA**

Grandpa Kingbury's Lowfat Chocolate Eclairs

Serves: 10 - 12

1 box lowfat graham crackers (Ralph's supermarket carries them)
1 (large) box lowfat vanilla or (1.5 ounce) instant pudding mix
3 cups nonfat milk
1 (12 ounce) container Fat Free Cool Whip, thawed
$1/_2$ can reduced fat chocolate frosting (Sweet Rewards brand)

Line the bottom of a 9" x 13" glass dish with a single layer of graham crackers. Combine pudding mix with milk in a large bowl and beat 75 seconds with electric mixer. Blend in Cool Whip and pour over graham cracker crust. Smooth over. Top with another layer of graham crackers. Frost with chocolate frosting, Cover with foil and place in refrigerator at least 4 hours. Remove from refrigerator just before serving and cut into squares.

"My dad, Bud Kingsbury, a B-17 Air Force pilot from World War II, got this recipe off a TV cooking show. It is low in calories and fat!"

Marianne Trew　　　　　　　　**Ball Junior High School, Anaheim, CA**

High-Fiber Cake

Serves: 10 - 12

$1/_2$ cup white northern beans, canned
1 cake mix, any flavor
2 eggs or 4 egg whites
1 $1/_4$ cups water

Preheat oven to 375 degree. Blend beans until smooth. Combine with remaining ingredients and beat 2 minutes. Pour into 2 greased and floured 8" cake pans. Bake 45 minutes. Test for doneness by inserting a toothpick in center. If it comes out clean, the cake is done.

"Both high fiber and low fat; makes a very soft, moist cake."

Rulene Jeffs　　　　　　　　**Kearns High School, Kearns, UT**

Light As Wind Cake

Serves: 9

4 eggs, separated
$2/_3$ cup water
1 $1/_2$ cups sugar
2 cups cake flour
1 teaspoon vanilla

Preheat oven to 375 degrees. Beat egg yolks and water until it makes a quart of liquid. Add sugar and beat 5 minutes. Add flour and vanilla. In separate bowl, beat egg whites until stiff. Fold into batter. Bake in tube cake pan for 30 minutes or until done.

"One of my grandmother's recipes. Great flavor and good for fruit shortcake."
Kathy Warren   **C.K. McClatchy High School, Sacramento, CA**

Light Lemon Squares

Serves: 16   *118 Cal; 3.2g Fat; 20.5g Carbs; 0.3g Fiber; 2.2g Protein; 68mg Sodium; 47mg Chol*

Crust:
1/4 cup granulated sugar
3 tablespoons butter or margarine, softened
1 cup flour
Topping:
3 eggs
3/4 cup granulated sugar
2 teaspoons lemon rind, grated
1/3 cup fresh lemon juice
3 tablespoons flour
1/2 teaspoon baking powder
1/8 teaspoon salt
2 teaspoons powdered sugar

Preheat oven to 350 degrees. To prepare crust, beat sugar and butter until creamy. Gradually add flour to sugar, beating at low speed until mixture resembles fine crumbs. Gently press mixture into bottom of an 8" x 8" squares baking pan. Bake 15 minutes; cool on wire rack. To prepare topping, beat eggs at medium speed until foamy. Add granulated sugar, lemon rind, lemon juice, flour, baking powder and salt. Beat until well blended. Pour mixture over partially baked crust. Bake 20 to 25 minutes or until set. Cool on wire rack. Sift powdered sugar evenly over top.

"Lower in fat and sugar than the original recipe, these are great!"
Penny Niadna   **Golden West High School, Visalia, CA**

Light 'n Luscious Cheesecake

Serves: 10   *180 Cal; 4g Fat; 18g Carbs; 7g Protein; 270mg Sodium; 20mg Chol*

3/4 cup graham cracker crumbs
2 tablespoons Mazola margarine, melted
1 cup lowfat cottage cheese
1 (8 ounce) container lowfat plain yogurt
1 (8 ounce) package light cream cheese
1/2 cup sugar
2 teaspoons orange peel, grated
2 teaspoons vanilla
2 egg whites

Preheat oven to 350 degrees. In a small bowl, combine graham cracker crumbs and margarine; pat into bottom of 8" springform pan. Bake 10 minutes. Remove from oven and lower heat to 325 degrees. Place cottage cheese in blender container; cover. Blend on high speed 2 minutes or until smooth. Add yogurt, cream cheese, sugar, orange peel and vanilla; blend until smooth. Add egg whites; blend until well mixed. Pour into prepared pan. Bake 30 minutes. Turn oven off and leave cheesecake in until cooled.

Betty Plooy   **Vanden High School, Fairfield, CA**

Low Carb Cheesecake

Serves: 12   *5.6g Carbs.*

32 ounces cream cheese, room temperature
6 eggs
2 cups whipping cream
1 vanilla bean, scraped
22 packets sugar substitute (Splenda)
4 tablespoons butter, melted

Preheat oven to 350 degrees. Wrap the bottom of a 9" springform pan in heavy-duty foil. Place all ingredients in a blender in 2 batches and blend 15 minutes. Pour both batches into a large bowl and stir gently. Pour mixture into springform pan. Place in a pan of hot water in oven. If water evaporates during baking, add more hot water, as needed. Bake 1 hour, turn off oven and leave cake in oven 1 hour more.

*"A delicious, rich, New York-style cheesecake that is so good
you won't miss the crust."*

Tisha Ludeman   **Brookhurst Junior High School, Anaheim, CA**

Low Carb Low Fat Lemon-Strawberry Bars

Serves: 16   *70 Cal; 3g Fat; 12g Carbs*

Crust:
$3/4$ cup Splenda or Stevia Sweetener
$3/4$ cup all-purpose flour
pinch salt
$1/4$ cup light butter
Filling:
1 $1/4$ cups Splenda or Stevia Sweetener
2 tablespoons all-purpose flour
$1/2$ cup egg substitute
$1/2$ cup half & half
$1/2$ cup fresh lemon juice
1 tablespoon fresh lemon peel, grated
$1/4$ cup reduced sugar strawberry preserves
fresh strawberries

Preheat oven to 350 degrees. Prepare crust: Spray a 8" x 8" baking pan generously with butter flavored nonstick spray; set aside. In medium bowl, mix Splenda or Stevia, flour and salt. Cut in light butter until mixture is crumbly, like a streusel topping. Do not overmix. Press dough into baking pan. Bake 15 to 20 minutes or until lightly browned. Prepare filling: Place Splenda or Stevia and flour in medium bowl; stir well. Add egg substitute and half & half; stir until blended. Stirring constantly, slowly add lemon juice and lemon peel. In a small bowl, stir preserves until smooth; spread evenly over warm crust. Gently pour lemon mixture over preserves. Bake 20 to 25 minutes or until set. Remove from oven and allow to cool before placing in refrigerator. Chill 2 hours in refrigerator before serving. Garnish with fresh strawberries.

*"The crumbly crust and sweet filling make these easy bars
a diet-wise party favorite!"*

Laura Zerpoli   **Monrovia High School, Monrovia, CA**

Lowfat Chocolate Chip Pumpkin Cookies

Makes: 2 dozen

1 box spice cake mix
1 (small) can pumpkin
1 cup miniature chocolate chips

Preheat oven to 350 degrees. Using an electric mixer, combine cake mix with canned pumpkin. Stir in chocolate chips. Drop dough onto ungreased cookie sheet and bake 8 to 9 minutes.

"This is a quick and easy treat that won't make you feel guilty! The pumpkin replaces most of the fat. Weight Watchers = 1 pt per cookie."

Jennifer Hill   **Kearns High School, Kearns, UT**

Lowfat Pumpkin Pie

Serves: 8   *3 points per serving*

4 sheets phyllo dough
$1/2$ cup dark brown sugar
$1/4$ teaspoon ground cloves
1 teaspoon cinnamon
1 teaspoon ground ginger
1 teaspoon cornstarch
$1/8$ teaspoon salt
1 $1/2$ cups canned pumpkin, puréed
1 $1/2$ cups fat free evaporated milk
$1/2$ cup egg substitute
1 teaspoon vanilla

Preheat oven to 350 degrees. Lightly coat a 9" round pie pan with nonstick cooking spray. Cut phyllo sheets in half. Place 1 sheet in prepared pan; lightly spray with cooking spray and top with another sheet of phyllo, placing corners just to the right of previous corners. Repeat with remaining sheets. Press phyllo into pan and roll in the edges. Bake until lightly browned, about 10 minutes. Whisk together brown sugar, spices, cornstarch and salt. In another bowl, whisk together pumpkin, evaporated milk, egg substitute and vanilla. Gradually whisk the wet ingredients into the dry ingredients. Pour filling into crust. Bake until set, about 50 minutes. Cover crust edges with foil if they start browning too quickly during baking. Cool completely before cutting.

"On Weight Watchers, this pie is only 3 points per serving."

Lura Staffanson   **Centennial High School, Corona, CA**

Mexican Cocoa Cake

Serves: 8   *227 Cal; 1g Fat*

    1 cup cake flour, sifted
    $1/3$ cup unsweetened cocoa powder
    1 teaspoon baking soda
    1 teaspoon baking powder
    1 teaspoon ground cinnamon
    6 (large) egg whites
    1 $1/3$ cups brown sugar, packed
    1 cup plain nonfat yogurt
    2 teaspoons vanilla
    $1/4$ teaspoon almond extract
    powdered sugar

In a small bowl, mix flour, cocoa, baking soda, baking powder and cinnamon. In a large bowl, beat egg whites, brown sugar, yogurt, vanilla and almond extract until well blended. Stir in flour mixture and beat just until evenly moistened. Pour batter into a greased 8" pan. Bake at 350 degrees until center of cake springs back when lightly pressed, about 30 to 40 minutes. Sprinkle top with powdered sugar. Serve warm or cooled.

"With only 1 gram of fat, this cake can satisfy one's sweet tooth without the worry of too much fat!"

Laura de la Motte   **Turlock High School, Turlock, CA**

Microwave Baked Apples

Serves: 2

    2 (large) cooking apples
    2 tablespoons brown sugar
    1 tablespoon raisins

Peel apples half way down and core about $3/4$ of the way down. Combine brown sugar and raisins in a small bowl. Pack the mixture into cored apples. Place in microwave safe bowls; cover and cook on 70%

power for 8 minutes, turning once halfway through the cooking time. Remove from microwave and let rest 5 minutes before serving.

Michelle Rutherford   **California State University, Fresno, CA**

No Guilt Oatmeal Cookies

Makes: 3 dozen

$1/_2$ cup Crisco
$1/_2$ cup brown sugar, firmly packed
$1/_4$ cup granulated sugar
$1/_2$ cup egg substitute OR 1 egg white
$1/_2$ teaspoon vanilla
$3/_4$ cup all-purpose flour
1 teaspoon baking soda
$1/_2$ teaspoon cinnamon
$1/_4$ teaspoon salt
1 $1/_2$ cups oats, uncooked
$1/_2$ cup raisins
$1/_2$ cup nuts, chopped

Preheat oven to 350 degrees. Beat Crisco and sugars until creamy. Add egg substitute and vanilla; beat well. Combine flour, baking soda, cinnamon and salt; add to creamed mixture, mixing well. Stir in oats, raisins and nuts, mix well. Drop by rounded tablespoons onto ungreased cookie sheet. Bake 10 to 12 minutes or until light golden brown.

"These are always a hit, and they are cholesterol free!"

Liz Aschenbrenner   **Sierra High School, Manteca, CA**

Oatmeal Crunchies

Makes: 24

4 tablespoons unsalted butter, softened
3 tablespoons sugar
2 tablespoons all-purpose flour
1 teaspoon vanilla
$1/_4$ teaspoon salt
$2/_3$ cup rolled oats

Preheat oven to 350 degrees; line two baking sheets with parchment paper. In medium bowl, mix butter with sugar, flour, vanilla and salt until smooth. Stir in rolled oats. Drop firmly packed teaspoon of dough 2" apart onto baking sheets. Bake 12 to 15 minutes, until golden, turning sheets halfway through baking. Cool on cookie sheet 1 minute; transfer to paper towels to cool completely.

Anna Monnich   **Lincoln High School, Stockton, CA**

Pineapple Angel Food Dessert

Serves: 10 - 12   *166 Cal; 0g Fat*

1 One-Step Angel Food Cake Mix
1 (20 ounce) can crushed pineapple
$1/4$ cup Grape Nuts cereal (optional)

Preheat oven to 350 degrees. Beat cake mix and crushed pineapple with juice in an extra large glass or metal bowl on low speed for 30 seconds. Beat on medium speed 1 minute. Pour into ungreased 9" x 13" pan and sprinkle with cereal, if desired. Bake 30 minutes, until top is golden brown and cracks feel very dry. Cool and serve with fat free whipped topping or strawberries.

Pamela Campion   **Dublin High School, Dublin, CA**

Pomegranate Sorbet

Serves: 4 - 6

$3/4$ cup + 1 tablespoon white sugar
$1/2$ cup water
2 teaspoons lemon juice
1 (15 ounce) bottle POM Pomegranate Juice or 2 cups fresh squeezed
Optional: Brut Champagne; fresh mint; pomegranate seeds

In a small saucepan, combine sugar with water; simmer syrup over moderate heat until thick and reduced to $3/4$ cup, approximately 5 minutes. Let cool to room temperature. Stir syrup and lemon juice into pomegranate juice. Transfer mixture into ice cream freezer and freeze according to manufacturer's instructions. While churning, chill a stainless steel bowl in freezer. When churning is done, transfer Sorbet to chilled bowl and serve.

"Pomegranate juice is dubbed the antioxidant super power.
Finally, a very healthy tasty dessert. Even better if topped with
champagne and a sprig of mint. Beautiful and yummy!"

Stephanie San Sebastian   **Central High School, Fresno, CA**

Pumpkin Roll

Serves: 24   *117 Cal; 3g Fat; 20g Carbs; 2g Protein*

> nonstick cooking spray
> flour
> 3 teaspoons powdered sugar, divided
> 3 (large) eggs
> 1 cup granulated sugar
> 3/4 cup self-rising cake flour
> 2/3 cup canned pumpkin pureé
> 2 teaspoons cinnamon
> 1 teaspoon ground ginger
> 1 teaspoon ground nutmeg
> 1 teaspoon vanilla
> 1 teaspoon fresh lemon juice
> *Icing:*
> 1 cup powdered sugar
> 1 (8 ounce) package Neufchatel cheese
> 1 teaspoon vanilla

Preheat oven to 325 degrees. Spray a jelly roll pan with nonstick cooking spray and sprinkle lightly with flour (or use parchment paper). Dust a clean dish towel with 1 teaspoon powdered sugar. Combine eggs, granulated sugar, flour, pumpkin, cinnamon, ginger, nutmeg, vanilla and lemon juice and beat well. Pour into pan and bake 15 minutes. Let cool 5 minutes, then invert onto dish towel. Sprinkle the cake with 1 teaspoon powdered sugar, then roll up jelly-roll style. Let cool. Cream the icing ingredients in a large bowl. Unroll cake, spread icing on top, then re-roll cake with the towel. Refrigerate until chilled. Sprinkle with remaining 1 teaspoon powdered sugar.

> *"This lowfat dessert was a hit a the Home Economics Teacher's Christmas party last year."*

Charlene Nugent   **Petaluma High School, Petaluma, CA**

Red, White & Blueberry Dessert

Serves: 6 - 8

> 3 to 4 baskets strawberries, halved or quartered
>   (save one whole for garnish)
> 2 baskets blueberries
> 2 jars marshmallow creme
> 2 (8 ounce) packages reduced fat cream cheese

Rinse and drain fruit, patting dry on paper towel to remove as much moisture as possible. Mix fruit together. In separate bowl, blend marshmallow creme with cream cheese until smooth; refrigerate mixture. In a clear class bowl, layer berries and cream cheese mixture.

Three layers looks great, ending with a large dollop of cream cheese mixture and one whole strawberry for garnish.

"This is a great 4th of July dessert or anytime in the summer when a lighter dessert is desired. Lowfat, delicious and easy!"

Renee Browning   **Hesperia High School, Hesperia, CA**

Silky Chocolate Mousse

Serves: 4   *370 Cal; 34g Fat; 22g Carbs; 7g Fiber; 60mg Sodium; 90mg Chol*

4 (1.1 ounce) bars Hershey's 1 Gram Sugar Carb Chocolate Candy
1 teaspoon unflavored gelatin
$1/2$ cup milk
$1/4$ cup Splenda
2 teaspoons vanilla
1 cup cold whipping cream

> Photo
> opposite
> page 129

Remove wrappers from candies. Break or cut into small pieces. Sprinkle gelatin over milk in small saucepan; let stand several minutes to soften. Cook over medium heat. stirring constantly until mixture just beings to boil. Remove from heat; immediately add chocolate candy, stirring until melted. Stir in Splenda and vanilla, blending until smooth. Pour into medium bowl; cool to room temperature. Beat whipping cream until stiff; gently fold into chocolate mixture just until combined. Refrigerate several hours. Garnish as desired

Hershey Kitchens   **Hershey, PA**

Strawberry Crepes

Serves: 8   *138 Cal; 28g Carbs; 6g Protein; 145mg Sodium; 1mg Chol*

1 $1/4$ cups fat free milk
$3/4$ cup Egg Beaters
1 teaspoon vanilla extract
1 cup flour
1 teaspoon sugar
$1/4$ teaspoon salt
$2/3$ cup strawberry Spreadable Fruit
3 cups fresh strawberries, chopped
2 teaspoons powdered sugar

In a blender, combine milk, egg substitute and vanilla. Blend 30 seconds. In separate bowl, combine flour, sugar and salt. Add to milk mixture and blend 2 minutes; stop and stir as necessary. Cover and refrigerate 1 hour. Use a nonstick 8" skillet and coat with nonstick cooking spray. Pour about 2 tablespoons batter into center; swirl pan to evenly coat bottom. Cook over medium heat until top is set, flip over and cook other side about 20 seconds. Repeat with remaining batter. You should have about 16 crepes. Spread each crepe with about 1 $1/2$

teaspoons spreadable fruit. Top with 3 tablespoons chopped strawberries. Roll up and lightly sprinkle with powdered sugar.

"Strawberries are a good source of Vitamin C, potassium, high fiber, fat free, low in calories and very low in sodium."

Dotti Jones   **Etiwanda High School, Rancho Cucamonga, CA**

Sugar-Free Oatmeal Cookies
Makes: 5 dozen   *3g Carbs; 4g Protein*

1 cup coconut oil
1 cup butter, room temperature
1 $1/_2$ cups Splenda
1 teaspoon molasses
2 eggs
1 teaspoon vanilla
$1/_2$ teaspoon salt
1 teaspoon baking soda
1 teaspoon cinnamon
1 cup rolled oats
1 cup pecans, chopped

Preheat oven to 350 degrees. With an electric mixer, beat together coconut oil, butter and Splenda until well blended, creamy and fluffy. Beat in molasses and eggs, combing well, followed by vanilla, salt and baking soda, scraping down sides of bowl a few times and making sure ingredients are well combined. Beat in cinnamon, rolled oats and pecans. Spray a cookie sheet with nonstick cooking spray and drop dough by tablespoonfuls onto cookie sheet leaving 2" to 2 $1/_2$" between cookies to allow for spreading. Bake 10 minutes, or until golden brown. Cool on cooling rack.

"Less carbohydrates and all the flavor!"

Nancy Patten   **Placerita Junior High School, Newhall, CA**

Sugar-Free Chocolate Mousse
Serves: 7   *7.5g Carbs; 1g Fiber; 4g Protein*

1 package chocolate sugar-free instant pudding mix
1 (10 ounce) package soft tofu
1 heaping tablespoon unsweetened cocoa powder
$1/_4$ to $1/_2$ teaspoon instant coffee crystals
1 $1/_2$ cups heavy whipping cream, chilled

Using an electric mixer, beat pudding mix with tofu, cocoa powder and coffee crystals until very smooth. In a separate bowl, whip cream until just about stiff. Turn the mixer to lowest setting, blend in the pudding mixture, then turn off mixer quickly! (If you overbeat, you will end up with chocolate butter!)

Nancy Patten   **Placerita Junior High School, Newhall, CA**

Swedish Cheesecake

Serves: 10 - 12

> 2 pounds nonfat cottage cheese
> 5 eggs, separated
> $1/2$ cup sugar
> 2 tablespoons + 2 teaspoons cornstarch
> 2 tablespoons + 2 teaspoons butter
> 2 teaspoons vanilla
> $2/3$ cup almonds, coarsely chopped, lightly toasted

Preheat oven to 350 degrees. In a food processor, process cottage cheese until smooth. Add egg yolks, sugar, cornstarch, butter and vanilla; process. *Optional:* Add 2 tablespoons of your favorite liqueur. Fold in almonds. Beat egg whites until stiff and fold into processed mixture. Pour filling into a greased 9" x 13" pan. Bake 50 to 60 minutes.

"Trader Joe's carries unsalted, dry, toasted, slivered almonds."

Becky Oppen   **Dana Hills High School, Dana Point, CA**

Tasty Lowfat Brownies

Makes: 24   *92 Cal; 2.1g Fat; 0.2g Fiber; 31mg Sodium; 18mg Cholesterol*

> nonstick cooking spray
> 1 $1/4$ cup unbleached flour
> $1/4$ teaspoon baking soda
> 1 $1/2$ cups sugar
> $1/3$ cup margarine
> $1/4$ cup buttermilk
> $3/4$ cup Dutch process cocoa
> 2 eggs
> 2 teaspoons vanilla

Heat oven to 350 degrees. Coat a 9" x 13" baking pan with nonstick spray. Whisk flour and baking soda in a bowl. Heat sugar, margarine and buttermilk, stirring constantly, in a saucepan over medium heat until mixture comes to a boil. Remove from heat and add cocoa. Stir until smooth. Cool 10 minutes. Add eggs, one at a time, to sugar mixture, stirring well after each addition. Add vanilla. Stir in flour mixture. Pour batter into pan. Bake 18-20 minutes, 'til done. Cool in pan on wire rack. Note: If you don't have buttermilk, you may substitute $1/4$ cup milk with $3/4$ teaspoon cider vinegar or lemon juice, microwave for 15 seconds.

"A tasty lowfat treat for chocolate lovers. "

Jean Adams   **Sonora High School, Sonora, CA**

Tofu Pie

Makes: 2 6" pies

> 1 egg white, beaten
> 2 (6") graham cracker pie crusts
> 1 (14 ounce) block Kinugoshi soft tofu
> 1 (3 ounce) box lime jello
> 1 (3 ounce) box lemon jello
> 2 cups hot water
> 1 (8 ounce) tub Cool Whip, thawed

Brush beaten egg white on pie crusts. Bake at 350 degrees for 5 minutes; let cool. Drain tofu thoroughly on paper towels. Cut into pieces and blend until liquefied, using food processor or blender. Dissolve jellos in hot water, then allow to cool a few minutes. Mix tofu into jello, then add Cool Whip; blend until smooth. Pour mixture into pie crusts. Refrigerate until set. Put on a dollop of Cool Whip before serving.

"Delicious! People cannot believe this is made with tofu!"

Reiko Ikkanda   **So. Pasadena Middle School, So. Pasadena, CA**

Unbelievable Pecan Pie (Sugar-Free)

Serves: 8

> 1 1/2 cups whole wheat flour, sifted
> 1 stick butter, softened
> 2 tablespoons butter, melted
> 3 eggs, beaten
> 1 cup Splenda
> 1 teaspoon vanilla
> 1 cup sugar free pancake syrup
> 1 1/2 cups pecans

Preheat oven to 350 degrees. Sift flour; cut in 1/4 cup softened butter and press into 8" or 9" pie pan. Refrigerate while preparing filling. Beat eggs; add Splenda, beat again. Add vanilla, remaining 2 tablespoons melted butter and syrup; mix well. Stir in pecans. Pour in refrigerated pie crust. Bake 45 minutes.

"A delicious, healthy dessert!"

Georgette Phillips   **Silverado High School, Victorville, CA**

Yummy Pancakes

Serves: 4

1 cup flour
2 eggs
$1/2$ teaspoon salt
1 teaspoon sugar
1 $1/2$ cups buttermilk
2 (large) apples, diced
nonstick cooking spray
Toppings: Powdered sugar, sour cream, apple sauce

In a large bowl, combine flour with eggs, salt, sugar, buttermilk and apples; mix well. (Batter will be thin.) Spray a skillet with nonstick cooking spray and heat over medium-high heat. Scoop batter onto hot skillet and fry until bubbles form round edges, turn over and cook until done. Serve hot with desired toppings.

"This is an old Russian recipe! Top with sour cream or applesauce or syrup. Kids love these thin, healthy pancakes!"

Victoria Brunn   **Lindbergh Educational Center, Manteca, CA**

Index Of CONTRIBUTORS

A

Abbey, Donna 30, 33
Pleasant Valley HS, Chico, CA

Adams, Jean 145
Sonora HS, Sonora, CA

Ali, Robin 82
Nevada Union HS, Grass Valley, CA

Allen, Barbara 68, 108
Ayala HS, Chino Hills, CA

Aschenbrenner, Liz 140
Sierra HS, Manteca, CA

Atkinson, Jeanette 28, 49
Cheyenne HS, Las Vegas, NV

B

Baczynski, Kathie 42, 63, 67, 88
Mt. Carmel HS, Poway, CA

Baker, Donna 93, 127
Redlands East Valley HS, Redlands, CA

Bankhead, Marilyn 35
San Marcos HS, San Marcos, CA

Bartholomew, Patti 84
Casa Roble HS, Orangevale, CA

Becker, Christine 41
Paradise IS, Paradise, CA

Bitner, LeeAnn 25
Alta HS, Sandy, UT

Black-Eacker, Ellen 8, 92
Nogales HS, La Puente, CA

Blanchette, Monica 51, 79
Landmark MS, Moreno Valley, CA

Bloemker, Beckie 104
Foothill HS, Sacramento, CA

Blough, Shirley 40
Hillside MS, Simi Valley, CA

Bolt, Rebecca 16, 107
Bear Creek HS, Stockton, CA

Bonilla, Pam 14, 66
Valley View HS, Moreno Valley, CA

Bottis, Dorene 89
Alvarado IS, Rowland Heights, CA

Brown, Angela 102
Sonora HS, Sonora, CA

Brown, Leah 69, 72
Marina HS, Huntington Beach, CA

Browning, Renee 143
Hesperia HS, Hesperia, CA

Brunn, Victoria 147
Lindbergh Educational Center, Manteca, CA

Bulat, Patty 77, 83
Rogers MS, Long Beach, CA

Burke, Brenda 59, 61
Mt. Whitney HS, Visalia, CA

Burnham, Jill 20, 62
Bloomington HS, Bloomington, CA

Burns, Priscilla 97
Pleasant Valley HS, Chico, CA

C

Cali, Mary Jo 35
Arroyo Grande HS, Arroyo Grande, CA

Call, Carole 68
Costa Mesa HS, Costa Mesa, CA

Campbell, Sue 44
Marsh JHS, Chico, CA

Campion, Pamela 5, 141
Dublin HS, Dublin, CA

Castro, Diane 124
Temecula Valley HS, Temecula, CA

Childers, Penny 52, 53
Ramona HS, Ramona, CA

Claiborne, Alice 7, 87
Fairfield HS, Fairfield, CA

Coffman, Mary 91
Reed HS, Sparks, NV

Coleman, Liz 11, 96
Oroville HS, Oroville, CA

Conner, Judy 8
Valley HS, Santa Ana, CA

Cooper, Lindy 34, 93
Simi Valley HS, Simi Valley, CA

Coots, Marie 50, 56
Huntington Beach HS,
Huntington Beach, CA

Croce, Angela 53, 122
Mira Mesa HS, San Diego, CA

Curfman, Astrid 14
Newcomb, Long Beach, CA

D

de la Motte, Laura 90, 139
Turlock HS, Turlock, CA

Dedini, Amy 80
Linden HS, Linden, CA

Deeton, Millie 30, 60
Ayala HS, Chino Hills, CA

Delap, Carole 42, 133
Golden West HS, Visalia, CA

Dobkins, Judy 5, 129
Redlands HS, Redlands, CA

Doig, Joyce 86
Ranchero MS, Hesperia, CA

Duffy, Therese 18
Warren HS, Downey, CA

Duncan, Wendy 36, 52
West Covina HS, West Covina, CA

E

Enright, Jill 83
Granite Hills HS, El Cajon, CA

Erickson, Sonja 43, 48, 115
Maria Carrillo HS, Santa Rosa, CA

Evans, Paulette 64
Cyprus HS, Magna, UT

Eyre, Julie 86, 88
Alhambra HS, Alhambra, CA

F

Farr, Debbie 24, 133
Foothill HS, Santa Ana, CA

G

Giauque, Laurie 27
Olympus HS, Salt Lake City, UT

Gordon, Ellen 46
Colton HS, Colton, CA

Greenwood, Debbie 75
Glendale HS, Glendale, CA

Greenwood, Gaylene 22, 101
Roy HS, Roy, UT

Grigg, Gayle 42
Hendrix JHS, Chandler, AZ

H

Harguess, LaRae 85
Hesperia HS, Hesperia, CA

Harvey, Debbie 120, 124
Amador Valley HS, Pleasanton, CA

Hawes, Anne 26
Cottonwood HS, Salt Lake City, UT

Hawkins, Kris 77, 113
Clovis West HS, Fresno, CA

Henderson, Gerry 91
Temple City HS, Temple City, CA

Henshaw, Barbara 40
Foothill HS, Pleasanton, CA

Henwood, Natalie 25, 126
Riverton HS, Riverton, UT

Herndon, Peggy 13
Central Valley HS, Shasta Lake City, CA

Hershey Kitchens 130, 131, 143
Hershey, PA

Hicks, Camille 7, 47, 61, 111
Riverton HS, Riverton, UT

Hill, Jennifer 37, 138
Kearns HS, Kearns, UT

Hitchens, Bree 21
El Modena HS, Orange, CA

Hobbs, Karyn 81
Lemoore HS, Lemoore, CA

Hogen, Kathie 63
Hendrix JHS, Mesa, AZ

Contributors

Hope, Sue 84, 115, 123
  Lompoc HS, Lompoc, CA

Hsieh, Linda 106
  Rowland HS, Rowland Heights, CA

Hughes, Sandy 99
  Upland HS, Upland, CA

I

Ikkanda, Reiko 55, 146
  So. Pasadena MS, So. Pasadena, CA

J

Jeffs, Rulene 85, 135
  Kearns HS, Kearns, UT

Johnson, Linda 87
  Riverbank HS, Riverbank, CA

Johnson, Pat 10, 70
  Iron Horse MS, San Ramon, CA

Jones, Dotti 50, 144
  Etiwanda HS, Rancho Cucamonga, CA

K

Kagy, Carol 132
  Norwalk HS, Norwalk, CA

Karapoulios, Eleni 122, 128
  Cypress HS, Cypress, CA

Katsilas, Christine 96, 120
  Taylorsville HS, Taylorsville, UT

Keane-Gruener, Mary 71
  Hoover HS, Glendale, CA

Kluever, Terry 69
  Coronado HS, Henderson, NV

Knowles, Gini 65
  Murrieta Valley HS, Murrieta, CA

Kras, Cheryl 22
  Saddleback HS, Santa Ana, CA

L

Landin, Bonnie 38
  Garden Grove HS, Garden Grove, CA

Lane-Hiltz, Julia 113, 114
  Durango HS, Las Vegas, NV

Langlois, Phyllis 17, 32
  Green Valley HS, Henderson, NV

Lawry's, Inc., ...98, 103, 104, 117
  Monrovia, CA

Lee, Deanna 41
  Marina HS, Huntington Beach, CA

Lee, Diana 109, 129
  David A. Brown MS, Wildomar, CA

Leighton, Beth 37
  Helix Charter HS, La Mesa, CA

Lewis, Laura 71
  Garden Grove HS, Garden Grove, CA

Ludeman, Tisha 137
  Brookhurst JHS, Anaheim, CA

Luna, Lori 48, 102
  Lemoore HS, Lemoore, CA

M

Marshall, Roberta 114
  Deer Valley HS, Antioch, CA

Marshman, Shirley 28
  West MS, Downey, CA

Massey, Sandra 6, 129
  Mt. View HS, El Monte, CA

Maurice, Sharron 44
  Blythe MS, Blythe, CA

McAuley, Gail 6, 115
  Lincoln HS, Stockton, CA

Melton, Kristi 62, 93
  Marina HS, Huntington Beach, CA

Miller, Cathy 63, 134
  Montclair HS, Montclair, CA

Molinaro, Adriana 39
  Granite Hills HS, El Cajon, CA

Monnich, Anna 140
  Lincoln HS, Stockton, CA

Montemagni, Maria 23
  Mt. Whitney HS, Visalia, CA

Montoy, Joanne 76, 134
  Esperanza HS, Anaheim, CA

Moyle, Cheryl 31, 67
  Olympus HS, Salt Lake City, UT

Murdoch, Cyndi 31
  Orland HS, Orland, CA

N

National Cattlemen's Beef Assoc. . .
  .74, 75, 78
  Chicago, IL

Newman, Libby 127
  West Valley HS, Hemet, CA

Niadna, Penny 136
  Golden West HS, Visalia, CA

Nugent, Charlene 58, 142
Petaluma HS, Petaluma, CA

O

Oppen, Becky 145
Dana Hills HS, Dana Point, CA

Owen, Laurie 27, 95
Challenger MS, San Diego, CA

P

Paolozzi, Laurie 56, 66
West HS, Torrance, CA

Patten, Nancy 144, 145
Placerita JHS, Newhall, CA

Pearl, Vicki 13
Townsend JHS, Chino Hills, CA

Peck, Pat 15
Folsom HS, Folsom, CA

Phillips, Georgette 14, 146
Silverado HS, Victorville, CA

Pittman, Holly 9, 58
El Capitan HS, Lakeside, CA

Plooy, Betty 98, 137
Vanden HS, Fairfield, CA

Poalillo, Val 116
Paso Robles HS, Paso Robles, CA

Policy, Janet 65
Ramona HS, Riverside, CA

R

Rabin-Fung, Betty 122
Sierra Vista JHS, Canyon Country, CA

Ramm, Venetta 47
La Habra HS, La Habra, CA

Ranger, Beverly 123
Carpinteria HS, Carpinteria, CA

Rosendahl, April 11, 89
Chino HS, Chino, CA

Runyan, Charlotte 110, 117
Saddleback HS, Santa Ana, CA

Rutherford, Michelle 119, 140
California State University , Fresno, CA

S

San Sebastian, Stephanie
. . . . .10, 36, 112, 141
Central HS, Fresno, CA

Saporetti, Deanna 77
Lemoore HS, Lemoore, CA

Sargent, Christina 92
Point Loma Nazarene Univ., San Diego, CA

Schaefer, Paula 127
Garside JHS, Las Vegas, NV

Schletewitz, Ruth 132
Rafer Johnson JHS, Kingsburg, CA

Schroeder, Ruth Anne 22, 49
River City HS, West Sacramento, CA

Schuette, Cheri 100, 130
Valley View MS, Simi Valley, CA

Schulenburg, Jan 9, 53
Irvine HS, Irvine, CA

Sheehan, Dale 121
Santana HS, Santee, CA

Shelburne, Julie 10, 94
Tulare Union HS, Tulare, CA

Sheridan, Cari 33
Grace Yokley MS, Ontario, CA

Silveira, Anne 6
Shasta HS, Redding, CA

Skrifvars, Paula 7
Brea JHS, Brea, CA

Smith, Delaine 62, 118
West Valley HS, Cottonwood, CA

Smith, Kelly 41, 96
Las Vegas HS, Las Vegas, NV

Smith, Pat 45, 85
Kern Valley HS, Lake Isabella, CA

Spencer, Debi 60, 79
Colton HS, Colton, CA

Spillman, Nancy 90
Lucerne Valley HS, Lucerne Valley, CA

Springhorn, Mary 112
Anderson HS, Anderson, CA

Staffanson, Lura 34, 139
Centennial HS, Corona, CA

Star, Victoria 54
McClatchy HS, Sacramento, CA

Steele, Carol 20
La Paz IS, Mission Viejo, CA

Stockdale, Daphne 38
Riverton HS, Riverton, UT

Stokes, Linda 23, 125
Riverton HS, Riverton, UT

Stroming, Patty 19, 44
Mitchell , Atwater, CA

Contributors

Swearingen, Myrna 50, 91
Corona HS, Corona, CA

Sweet-Gregory, Jill 57
Santa Paula HS, Santa Paula, CA

T

Topp, Judith 73, 80
A. B. Miller HS, Fontana, CA

Traw, Marianne 105, 135
Ball JHS, Anaheim, CA

Tresley, Shelly 29
McQueen HS, Reno, NV

Truitt, Debby 64, 106
Woodland HS, Woodland, CA

Tuttle, Jan 12, 70
Mills HS, Millbrae, CA

Tyree, Sonja 12, 55
Ayala HS, Chino Hills, CA

U

Urquidi, Rita 47
Nogales HS, La Puente, CA

V

Verdi, DeeAnn 31, 110
North Valleys HS, Reno, NV

W

Warren, Kathy 136
C.K. McClatchy HS, Sacramento, CA

Waterbury, Sue 18
San Luis Obispo HS, San Luis Obispo, CA

Webb, Melissa 100
Lakewood HS, Lakewood, CA

Wells, Betty 113
Bidwell JHS, Oroville, CA

Williams, Jackie 19, 35
Prospect HS, Saratoga, CA

Wilson, Lori 100
A.B. Miller HS, Fontana, CA

Winter, Carol 16
Hillcrest HS, Midvale, UT

Wisconsin Milk Marketing Board
.....................45, 57
Madison, WI

Wolak, Diane 51
Martin Luther King HS, Riverside, CA

Y

Young, Shauna 65, 101
Jordan HS, Sandy, UT

Z

Zerpoli, Laura 138
Monrovia HS, Monrovia, CA

Index Of RECIPES

Appetizers & Beverages

Chunky Artichoke Salsa 5
Chunky Black Bean Salsa 5
Crab Tostadas 6
Dill Vegetable Dip 6
Fruit Smoothie 6
Fruity Freeze .7
Fruity Tofu Shakes 7
Hot Feta Artichoke Dip 7
Judy's Berry Smoothie 8
Kary's Aunt Lisa's Cheese Spread 8
Lite Shrimp Spread 8
Mac's Olive Hummus 9
Mango Smoothie 9
Mango-Ade .10
Pickled Shrimp 10
Pineapple Cooler 11
Portabello and Cheese Bruschetta 11
Spinach-Artichoke Dip 12
Spinach-Stuffed Mushrooms 12
Tangy Meatballs 13
Tomato, Basil & Cheese Kabobs 13
Tropical Sunset Punch 13
Turkey Wontons 14
Zesty Dressing & Dip 14

Breads & Baked Items

Banana Bread (Low Sugar) 15
Best Bran Muffins 15
Bran Flax Muffins 16
Golden Harvest Muffins 17
Granola 17
Healthy Banana Nut Bread 18
Honey Wheat Muffins 18
Lemon Blueberry Muffins 19
Low Fat Blueberry Muffins 19

Lowfat Biscuits 20
Lowfat Doughnuts 21
Lowfat Poppy Seed Muffins 21
Marvelous Muffins 22
Oat & Apricot Breakfast Bars 22
Pumpkin-Carrot Muffins 23
Raisin Bran Muffins 23
Refrigerator Bran Muffins 24
Spiced Pumpkin Bread 24
Wake-Up Cake 25

Soups, Stews & Chili

Black Bean and Salsa Soup 26
Canned Cream Soup Substitute 26
Cheddar Chicken Chowder 27
Chicken Soup Parmigiana 28
Chicken Tortilla Soup 28
Chili Turkey with White Beans 29
Chinese Chicken Noodle Soup 29
Crab and Asparagus Soup 30
Cream of Broccoli Soup 30
Fiesta Soup .31
Grandma's Beef Vegetable Soup 31
Hamburger Minestrone 32
Herbed Cucumber Soup
  with Toasted Almonds 32
Italian Potato Soup 33
Low Calorie Vegetable Soup 33
Lowfat Mexican Soup 34
Luscious Lentil Soup 34
Sassy Black Bean Soup 35
Shrimp Corn Chowder 35
Shrimp Creole Stew 36
Stracciatella (Italian Wedding Soup) . .36
Tortilla Soup 37
Turkey Taco Soup 37

Eating BETTER

Salads, Slaws & Dressings

24-Hour Fruit Salad 38
Apple Cole Slaw 38
Autumn Salad 39
Caribbean Potato Salad 39
Cheese & Peas Salad 40
Chicken Cabbage Salad 40
Chicken Salad 41
Chicken Salad 41
Chilled Asparagus Dijon Salad 42
Confetti Salad 42
Cranberry Jello Salad 42
Cranberry Nut Salad 43
Crisp Spinach Salad 43
Cucumbers in Yogurt 44
Fruit & Yogurt Salad 44
Fruited Chicken Salad 45
Go-Go Wisconsin
  Blue Cheese Apple Walnut Salad 45
Greek Salad - Village Style 46
Greek Salad w/Lemon Dressing 46
Green Salad with Orange Dressing . . .47
Jalapeño Dressing 47
Jicama & Carrot Salad 48
Jicama, Orange & Cilantro Salad 48
Lowfat Jello Pretzel Salad 49
Lowfat Macaroni Salad 49
Mandarin Raspberry Salad 50
Mango Raspberry Salad 50
Oriental Cabbage Salad 50
Oriental Greens Salad 51
Quick & Easy Elegant Salad 51
Raspberry Mango Salad 51
Salad with Avocado Dressing 52
Spinach Salad
  with Raspberry Dressing 52
Springtime Salad 53
Summer Strawberry Chicken Salad . . .53
Tabouli with a Twist 54
Tofu Salad 54
Un-Potato Salad 55

Sauces, Salsas & Marinades

Cilantro Dipping Sauce 56
Easy Marinade 56
Honey Yogurt Sauce 57
Italian Sauce 57
Mango Salsa 57
Peach & Mango Salsa 58

Vegetables & Side Dishes

Beets with Orange & Ginger 59
Brown Rice Primavera 60
Creamy Cauliflower-Pea Medley 60
Eggplant Italian Style 61
Fabulous French Fries 61
Fantastic Fruit with Yogurt Dressing . .61
Greek Omelet 62
Green Beans & Feta with Dill 62
Guacamole .63
Italian Vegetables 63
Lemon Herb Broccoli 63
Lowfat Potato Casserole 64
Mashed Cauliflower 64
No Fry French Fries 64
Quick and Easy
  Marinated Green Beans 65
Refrigerator Pickles 65
Roasted Vegetable Medley 66
Sautéed Apples & Squash 66
Spanish Rice 67
Stuffed Tomatoes 67
Sugar Snap Peas 68
Tangy Lime Risotto 68
Tomatoes in Basil
  & Balsamic Vinegar 69
Twice Baked Squash 69
Unfried Cheese Fries 70
Vegetable Casserole 70
Vegetable Frittata 71
Vegetable Garden Medley 71
Zucchini and Tomato Gratin 72

Main Dishes: Beef

Beef Stroganoff 73
Beef Stuffed Peppers 74
Easy Beef Steak Diane 74
Fajitas 75
Lite Taco Salad 76
Low Calorie Quickie Calzone 76
Mexican Beef Stew 77
Roast Beef with Bleu Cheese Salad . . .77
Sesame Soy Beef Stir Fry 78
Shredded Beef Sandwiches 78
Stuffed Peppers 79
Stuffed Shells 79
Veal Cutlets a la Vegetables 80
Zucchini Lasagna 81

Recipes

Main Dishes: Poultry

Apple Chicken and Rice 82
Asian Chicken Wraps 82
Bacon Chicken 83
Barbecued Chicken Quesadillas 83
Basil Chicken Vermicelli 84
Caesar Chicken 84
Chicken and Pasta with Salsa 85
Chicken Asparagus Fajitas 85
Chicken & Asparagus Roll-Up 86
Chicken Fajita Burritos 86
Chicken Fingers 86
Chicken, Mushroom
  & Broccoli Casserole 87
Chicken Picante 87
Chicken Tacos 88
Chicken Vegetable Stir Fry 88
Chile Chicken Stack 89
Citrus Chicken 89
Citrus Herb Roasted Chicken 90
Crockpot Chili 90
Dash Diet Mexican Bake 91
Easy Chicken in Wine Sauce 91
Ellen's Honey Mustard Chicken 92
Garlic Teriyaki Chicken 92
Gourmet Chicken Breasts 92
Greek Chicken 93
Green Enchilada Chicken Casserole . . .93
Grilled Chicken & Nectarine Salad . . .94
Grilled Chicken with Fruit Salsa 95
Healthy Chicken Taco Salad 95
Italian Style Turkey Cutlets 96
Lemon Linguine 96
Lowfat Chicken Caesar Salad 97
Lowfat Tacos 98
Mesquite Chicken Kabobs 98
Mexi Chili Mac 99
Oriental Barbecued Chicken 99
Parmesan Chicken 100
Philly Cheese Chicken Wrap 100
Pineapple Chicken Stir-Fry 101
Quick Southwest Chicken
  and Black Bean Skillet 101
Salsa Chicken 102
Santa Fe Chicken 102
Southwest Citrus Chicken
  with Corn Salsa 103
Southwestern Chicken Salad 103

Stuffed Chicken Parmigiana 104
Swiss Chicken Cutlets 105
Turkey Sloppy Joes 105
Turkey Veggie Meatballs 106
Turkey with Black Bean Salsa 107

Main Dishes: Pork

5 Spice Grilled Pork with
  Sweet & Sour Orange Glaze 108
Deep Dish Quiche Pizza 109
Pork Tenderloin
  with Orange Marmalade 109
Spicy Pork Chops 110

Main Dishes: Seafood

Cilantro Salmon Bake 111
Grilled Sea Bass 111
Halibut Mexican-Style 112
Halibut with Relish 112
Honey Glazed Salmon 113
One Pot Dinner - Shrimp 113
One Pot Dinner - Tuna 113
Pan Fried Catfish 114
Pasta and Garlic-Lemon Tuna
  Sauce w/Capers & Parsley 114
Salmon on the Grill 115
Salmon Steaks with
  Grilled Red Onion Slices 115
Scallops & Bell Peppers
  over Whole Wheat Linguine 116
Seafood Enchiladas 116
Teriyaki Salmon with Fresh Pineapple
  Salsa 117
Teriyaki Salmon 118

Main Dishes: Meatless

10 Minute Chili 119
Hearty Multi-Bean Chili 119
Lowfat Stuffed Shells 120
Mexican Black Bean Chili 120
Mushroom Lasagna 121
Peggy's Garden Fettuccini 121
Spinach & Mushroom Frittata 122
Sweet Yellow Peppers
  & Tomatoes with Feta Cheese 122
Tomato Basil Pasta 123
Vegan Veggie Rice Bowl 123
Vegetable Quiche 124
Vegetable Pizza with
  Fantastic Pizza Crust 125

Desserts

Almond Cookies 126
Almond Joy Pie 126
Angel Food DeLight 127
Angel Food Pineapple Cake 127
Apple Crumble 128
Banana Pudding 128
Cafe Latte Custard 129
Cheesecake Cupcakes 129
Cheesecake Pudding 130
Chocolate Bits Cheesecake 130
Chocolate Cream Brownie Torte 131
Chocolate-Orange Hazelnut Biscotti .131
Cinnamon Sugar Cookie Twists 132
Debbie's Sugar Free Apple Pie 133
Fancy Frozen Fruit Cups 133
Floating Fruit Parfait 134
French Silk Pie 134
Grandpa Kingbury's
  Lowfat Chocolate Eclairs 135
High Fiber Cake 135
Light As Wind Cake 135
Light Lemon Squares 136
Light 'n Luscious Cheesecake 136
Low Carb Cheesecake 137
Low Carb Low Fat
  Lemon-Strawberry Bars 137
Lowfat Chocolate Chip
  Pumpkin Cookies 138
Lowfat Pumpkin Pie 138
Mexican Cocoa Cake 139
Microwave Baked Apples 139
No Guilt Oatmeal Cookies 140
Oatmeal Crunchies 140
Pineapple Angel Food Dessert 141
Pomegranate Sorbet 141
Pumpkin Roll 142
Red, White & Blueberry Dessert 142
Silky Chocolate Mousse 143
Strawberry Crepes 143
Sugar Free Oatmeal Cookies 144
Sugar-Free Chocolate Mousse 144
Swedish Cheesecake 145
Tasty Lowfat Brownies 145
Tofu Pie 146
Unbelievable Pecan Pie (Sugar Free) .146
Yummy Pancakes 147

For additional copies of *this* book,
and our *other* cookbook titles,
please visit our website:

www.creativecookbook.com

Or, use the re-order forms below.

Eating BETTER ▌**C**REATIVE **C**ookbook

Please send me _____ copy(ies) of *Eating Better* at **$12.00** each.
(includes tax and postage). Make checks payable to:
Creative Cookbook Company, 6292 Newbury Dr., Huntington Beach, CA 92647

Enclosed is my check for _____ book(s) at **$12.00** each $_____.

Name _____

Address _____

City _____ State _____ Zip _____

Eating BETTER ▌**C**REATIVE **C**ookbook

Please send me _____ copy(ies) of *Eating Better* at **$12.00** each.
(includes tax and postage). Make checks payable to:
Creative Cookbook Company, 6292 Newbury Dr., Huntington Beach, CA 92647

Enclosed is my check for _____ book(s) at **$12.00** each $_____.

Name _____

Address _____

City _____ State _____ Zip _____